Traditional Quilts
for Kids to Make

BARBARA J. EIKMEIER

Martingale™
& COMPANY

Woodinville, Washington

Dedication

To my teachers and my students:
I have learned something from each of you.

Acknowledgments

Thank you to Gayle Snitselaar, of Benartex Fabrics, for providing fabric that was used in pattern testing blocks and sample quilts, including *Cousins by the Row* (page 55).

Many children and adults tested patterns and made quilts for this book. Thank you to: Sarah Bryant; Rachel Capra; Ashley Carmichael; Caroline Cronin; Eric Eikmeier; Sarah Eikmeier; Nicole Gonder; Anna Martin; Becky Martin and her aunt, Carol Martin; David Martin; Kate Mock and her mother, Tracy Mock; Christopher and Steven Nieto and their mother, Karen Nieto; and Patrick and Robert Rielly and their mother, Anne Rielly.

Karen Hayes, of Fort Campbell High School, Fort Campbell, Kentucky, led her students in pattern testing each design in "The Block Workshop" (page 18). Special thanks to her and to the students who participated: Shawana Adams, Rebekah Britt, Rachel Gouge, Erin Haase, Sheena McAlpine, Stepanie McMahon, Crystal Patterson, Sarah Waddell, and Suzanne Waddell.

And most of all, thank you to my family. My husband, Dale, deserves a medal for patience and understanding, as do my children, Eric and Sarah.

Credits

President . . . . Nancy J. Martin
CEO . . . . Daniel J. Martin
Publisher . . . . Jane Hamada
Editorial Director . . . . Mary V. Green
Editorial Project Manager . . . . Tina Cook
Design and Production Manager . . . . Stan Green
Technical Editor . . . . Karen Soltys
Copy Editor . . . . Chris Rich
Illustrators . . . . Laurel Strand, Jil Johänson, Lisa McKenney
Photographer . . . . Brent Kane
Cover Designer . . . . Stan Green
Interior Design . . . . Jennifer LaRock Shontz

Traditional Quilts for Kids to Make
© 2001 by Barbara J. Eikmeier

Martingale & Company
20205 144th Ave. NE
Woodinville, WA 98072-8478
www.martingale-pub.com

Printed in Canada
06 05 04 03 02 01   8 7 6 5 4 3 2 1

Mission Statement

We are dedicated to providing quality products and service by working together to inspire creativity and to enrich the lives we touch.

Library of Congress Cataloging-in-Publication Data

Eikmeier, Barbara J.
    Traditional quilts for kids to make / Barbara J. Eikmeier.
        p. cm.
    ISBN 1-56477-353-1
    1. Patchwork—Patterns. 2. Machine quilting—Patterns.
    I. Title: Subtitle on spine: Traditional quilts for kids to
    make. II. Title.
TT835.E44 2001
746.46—dc21   00-065358

Contents

Preface

Years ago, on a small military post in the Mojave Desert, I began teaching children how to quilt. At first, we sewed small quilted items such as pillows and little quilts. While the children loved these small projects, the inevitable soon happened: They discovered big quilts! Before long, they wanted to make quilts large enough to sleep under.

Initially, I presented my students with the cut pieces for 12" blocks. The students arranged the pieces as if they were assembling jigsaw puzzles and then sewed them together to create the blocks. I soon realized, however, that the simpler the blocks were and the less time it took to finish them, the more successful and satisfied the students were. As a result, I started to adapt block patterns so the blocks contained fewer seams, and I also taught the students shortcut techniques. The children were confused at first because these techniques—sewing with quick triangles and folded corners—made it difficult for them to see a block's design until they'd constructed at least a portion of the block. Soon, however, the children were calling this new process "magic." They grew to love the fact that as they sewed, cut, and pressed—voilà!—like magic, the block patterns emerged.

At the time, more than thirty-five students were attending my weekly quilting classes, and some had been attending for more than two years. Coming up with new things for them to sew was a continual challenge. The patterns presented in my first book, *Kids Can Quilt*, were designed for these students. However, the patterns in this book actually came first!

Leftovers by Caroline Cronin, age 12, 2000, Seoul, South Korea. See "Using Leftovers" on page 13 to learn how the quilts on this page were made.

Leftovers by Nicole Gonder, age 13, 2000, Seoul, South Korea.

Introduction

In *Kids Can Quilt*, I shared my concept of quilting as a partnership. I've continued with that concept in this new book. Although many children will eventually become independent quiltmakers, I firmly believe that if experienced quiltmakers rotary cut the pieces and draw sewing lines for beginners, children can piece as accurately as many adults. Of course, some of the students who tested patterns for this book became independent sewers. Karen Hayes, a high school home economics teacher in Kentucky, reported that several students who pattern tested came to her for help only when they didn't understand something in the written directions. Rachel Gouge, an independent student, pattern tested several of the blocks and did all of her own cutting and sewing.

Accurately cut and accurately sewn patches should match up perfectly. The truth, however, is that we aren't always accurate in both arenas, so we need to be flexible at certain points. My philosophy about students and accuracy is this: I want my students to love quilting. If I make them rip every seam that isn't perfect, I decrease my chances of creating new lovers of quilts. Instead of forcing students to rip seams, I often teach them about easing. (You'll find easing instructions on page 16.) My students are wonderful at easing!

When I asked ten-year-old Kate Mock if she would pattern test for this book, she hesitated when she learned how large the proposed quilt would be. Her mother, Tracy Mock, said to her, "You can do it. The blocks are big and the pieces in each block are big, too." In an adult quilting world filled with little, perfect pieces and tiny, perfect stitches, helping a child learn to quilt with big pieces and big blocks brings much joy. Kate astonished both her mother and me with her sampler quilt; she proudly created *Follow the Yellow Brick Road* (page 58), a quilt large enough to sleep under.

I grew up in a 4-H family, so getting ready for the fashion review and county fair are etched in my memory of childhood. Also etched in my memory is the fact that I had to complete all the work by myself. For years, I wanted my young students to do all their own work, too. I knew they could, and I was committed to teaching them to follow through on finishing the projects they started. Then reality sank in. Just as adults have favorite quilting tasks, so do children. Many children love to piece, especially on a sewing machine, but most aren't wild about quilting, and usually, they don't care much for hand stitching the bindings in place. I've taken these facts into consideration and have modified my stance on finishing projects; I now allow adults to help with quilting and finishing. Being helped doesn't diminish the children's pride in their work; in fact, they're all the more proud to have participated in a successful partnership and to have a finished quilt.

If your students get help finishing their quilts, teach them to share the credit by having them include the appropriate information on labels attached to the backs of the quilts. Of course, if a project will be an entry in a judged or graded event, make sure all the entrance requirements are met; these requirements may preclude a child's getting help with the actual sewing.

No matter who finishes a quilt—a student, a mom, or a willing neighbor—the important part of creating a quilt is having fun. When you have fun teaching your child or a group of quilting students, they'll also learn to have fun making quilts. And that's the whole point!

Using This Book

Traditional Quilts for Kids to Make is arranged like a menu. Students can start by turning to "The Block Workshop" (pages 18–38) and choosing the designs they wish to sew. Then they can move to "Settings" (pages 39–44) and select an arrangement for their blocks. Finally, they can turn to "Finishing Your Quilt" (pages 72–78) at the back of the book and pick a finishing method. Of course, if students like, they can work through the book in a different order. For example, they might want to choose their settings first and then decide which blocks to include.

MAKING PROJECT CUE CARDS

Because the layout of this book requires flipping back and forth from section to section, your students may find it helpful to make "cue cards" with page numbers on them for quick reference. Here's a sample format for a cue card:

Block Name
   (or Names): _____ Page: _____

Special Techniques: _____ Page: _____

Setting Name: _____ Page: _____

Borders: _____ Page: _____

Edge Finishing: _____ Page: _____

Quilting: _____ Page: _____

If students want to create their own quilt plans, they'll need help calculating yardage and creating cutting charts. (These aren't difficult tasks once you know what a given quilt plan requires.) Several of the students whose work is shown in this book adapted plans and modified instructions to make the quilts they wanted. Thirteen-year-old Nicole Gonder saw a picture of ten-year-old Patrick Rielly's *Fall Leaves* quilt (page 54). She liked the repetitiveness of the leaf design, but she preferred the butterfly pattern, so she used it to make *Butterflies II* (page 52). Sarah Bryant didn't want to use more than six block patterns in her quilt, *Sarah's Sampler* (page 69). She wanted to make her quilt larger, though, so she made the six blocks and then reversed their color placement and repeated them. Sarah Eikmeier wanted a lot of different patterns for her *Patch Quilt* (page 62), but only two patterns in "The Block Workshop" (page 18) included the large center squares that she liked. To increase the variety in her quilt, Sarah made four different blocks from two patterns by changing the corners of one pattern and the colors and arrangement of another.

Certain blocks work better for specific settings. When using the "Next to Each Other" and "Row by Row" settings (pages 44 and 43), students should consider which parts of their blocks will end up touching other blocks—and where. Some blocks, such as the Flag (page 20), can be adapted by changing the color placement, as in *Follow the Yellow Brick Road* (page 58). If you join the House blocks (page 23) in a horizontal row, the houses may blur together visually. Instead, try alternating houses, making some with sky and some with grass. The alternating positions of the grass and sky pieces stagger the placement of the houses.

In some instances, the blocks may look fine when they're arranged next to each other, but their seams are pressed the wrong way, and sewing them together is difficult. When Becky Martin made *Becky's Stars* (page 46), she consistently pressed the seams toward the blue fabric. When she set the blocks together, the seams automatically ran in opposite directions.

If you keep all these concerns in mind, you'll be able to help your students make the right decisions about their quilts.

Tools and Supplies

 Rest assured that your students will be eager to get started. Everyone will work more successfully and have more fun, however, if you're all well prepared.

Sewing Kits

Students should have their own sewing kits. Resealable plastic bags work well as containers. Each kit should contain the following tools and supplies:

Pincushion. Teach the kids from the beginning to "park" their needles and pins in pincushions.

Straight pins. I use Dritz extra-fine glasshead pins when I teach kids. Their heads are easy for children to pick up and hold, and their sharp points slip easily through fabric.

Needles. My all-time favorite needles for kids are Piecemakers embroidery needles, size 7. I like these needles because their eyes are large enough for kids to thread easily and because I find that these needles resist bending. My students use them both to hand piece and hand quilt.

MAKING NEEDLES LAST LONGER

Kids have hot little hands that seem to wear the chrome off the needles they use. Running the needles through a strawberry emery will help keep them clean and sharp. Encouraging the kids to wash their hands before and during class also seems to help.

Scissors. Give your kids scissors that cut! My students use Fiskars for Kids, with the pointed tip. Although these wonderful scissors are sharp enough to cut fabric and thread well, they're blunt enough for children to handle safely and are perfectly suited for a child's sewing kit.

¼" seamer. Children can use this handy tool to measure ¼"-wide seam allowances on pieces that you rotary cut for them. I let the kids try the several styles that I own and pick the ones they like using best. The Add-a-Quarter™ ruler is often a favorite.

Pencil and sharpener. Children find it easier to piece when they have marked lines to sew on.

Sewing and quilting thread. Children deserve the best 100-percent cotton sewing thread available. High-quality thread made from long cotton fibers resists knotting and tangling. I've had the best results with Mettler Swiss Metrosene. Tan or medium gray are good color choices for piecing. Many brands of quilting thread are available; just choose one that doesn't tangle easily. A variety of colors is nice; kids love color. Some of my students like to change colors every time they rethread their needles!

Other Necessities

The space in which your students will work should include the following equipment, tools, and supplies:

Sewing machine. Your sewing machine should be in good working order. Make sure the manual is available; your students will need to refer to it from time to time.

Rotary cutter, cutting mat, and ruler. All three of these items are necessary for rotary cutting. My favorite ruler is 6" x 12" and has a 1" grid and ⅛" gradations. (A ⅛" increment is quite common in quilting.) A Bias Square® ruler, which includes a 45-degree angle mark, is useful when you're cutting fabric strips on the bias.

Sandpaper board. Available at quilt shops, sandpaper boards help keep fabric from slipping while you're drawing sewing lines. To make your own board, just glue fine-grit sandpaper to firm sheets of cardboard.

Safety pins. One-inch safety pins are great for pinning long seams and triangle patches. Kids can also use safety pins to pin-baste their quilt layers for machine quilting.

Seam ripper. Like most adults, kids don't enjoy picking out stitches. The method they seem to find least traumatic is to break every fourth or fifth stitch by catching it with a seam ripper. After breaking intermittent stitches along the seam, the children can turn the sewing over, loosen the thread on the back, and tug gently to release the whole row of stitching.

Iron and ironing board. Teach your students to press seams as they go. See "Pressing" (page 14).

Old spoon. This comes in handy during hand quilting. See pages 72–73 for details.

Fabric. I use and recommend 100-percent cotton fabric in a variety of prints and solids because cotton is easiest for children to handle, iron, and stitch. I let the students choose their own fabrics, but I offer them guidance to help them achieve contrast between colors. Yardage calculations are based on 40" of usable width, which allows for shrinking and removing of the tightly woven selvages. The fabric you use may actually be wider, in which case you'll sometimes have leftover strips. With my students, I refer to the right side of the fabric as the "bright side" and the wrong side as the "dull side." (Solids and woven plaids do not have right and wrong sides.)

Batting. I've experimented with a variety of battings and get the nicest results with 80-percent cotton/20-percent polyester batting. The blanket-like quality of this batting helps the quilt layers stick together, which makes handling it easier than handling 100-percent polyester batting, especially when you're machine quilting.

Basic Techniques

 In this section, you'll find descriptions of the basic techniques you'll need to know in order to teach children successfully, from cutting fabric to assembling and joining pieces.

Cutting Fabric

As the adult partner in this endeavor, it's your job to cut the required pieces with rotary-cutting equipment. Although I teach older students to handle this equipment safely when they do their own cutting, I prefer to do all the cutting for the younger students prior to the sewing session. Be sure the younger students know that they should never handle the rotary cutter. This wonderful tool can be very dangerous when used improperly.

1. Press any wrinkles out of the fabric. Fold the fabric in half from selvage to selvage; then fold it in half again, aligning the first fold and the selvages. (Some quiltmakers prefer to fold the fabric in half only once and then straighten the edge. Use whichever method you prefer.)

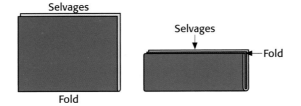

2. Position the fabric on the cutting mat and align a Bias Square ruler or another ruler with the bottom fold. Slide the ruler toward the left-hand edge of the folded fabric, making sure that all 4 layers are underneath the ruler.

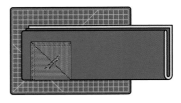

3. Position a rotary ruler so that it rests evenly against the edge of the Bias Square ruler. Remove the Bias Square ruler and cut along the right-hand edge of the rotary ruler. To make a clean, straight cut, press down firmly and evenly on the rotary cutter. Discard this fabric trimming.

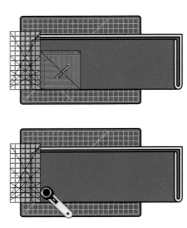

4. Align the required measurement on the ruler with the cut edge of the fabric and cut a fabric strip. Repeat to cut the number of strips you need. (After cutting a few of these strips, straighten the fabric edge again if necessary by repeating steps 1–3.)

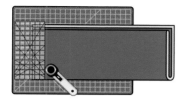

5. Cut off and discard the tightly woven selvage on the ends of each strip. Then crosscut the strips into squares or rectangles, following the instructions that accompany your selected blocks.

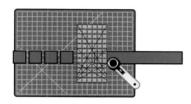

6. Occasionally, you may need strips that are wider than your ruler. A large, square ruler comes in handy for this purpose. If you don't have one, cut these wide strips by using the measurement marks on your cutting mat. After straightening the fabric edge, slide the fabric to the "0" line on your mat and align the folded edge of the fabric with a straight line on the mat. Using the measurements across the top of the mat, measure and cut the strip.

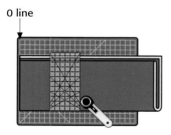

0 line

Ensuring Accurate Seams

I use two basic methods to measure seam allowances with my students: I either draw sewing lines for them, or I place a marker on the sewing-machine bed to serve as a seam guide. Drawing sewing lines takes more time, but some students never master using a marker as a seam guide. Try both methods with your students, and let them choose the one that suits them best. Remember: Drawing sewing lines is worth your time if it helps a child learn to love quilting.

Drawing Sewing Lines

Draw a sewing line on the wrong side of only one fabric piece in each pair of fabric pieces. Lines on both pieces may create confusion, and they aren't necessary as long as your students pin the pieces accurately. Many of my older students have successfully learned to draw lines for themselves. Encourage the children to try, but think of drawing lines as one of your jobs in the quilting partnership.

To draw a sewing line:
1. Place the fabric wrong side up on a sandpaper board. The sandpaper will stabilize the fabric.
2. Position the Add-a-Quarter ruler or another accurate marking tool on the fabric, so that one edge is parallel to the edge of the fabric and overlaps the fabric by ¼".

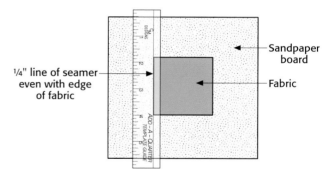

¼" line of seamer even with edge of fabric

Sandpaper board

Fabric

3. With a sharp pencil, draw a sewing line on the fabric along the edge of the ruler.

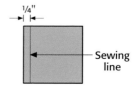

¼"

Sewing line

Placing a Marker

If your students will be machine sewing, another good way to mark a sewing line is to place some sort of marker on the bed of the machine. A number of materials work well. Adhesive-backed moleskin can be cut to size, and because this material is thick, it provides a raised ridge against which the fabric can be moved. Stacked strips of masking tape serve the same purpose. The most original seam marker I've ever seen was a Band-Aid. My student, Rachel Capra, came to class with one already in place on her machine. Band-Aids come in great designs, and their little pads create a ridge for the fabric to follow, while the flat tabs lie smooth against the machine bed. Try several materials to find your favorite.

To place the marker properly:
1. Place a sheet of ¼"-grid graph paper under the presser foot of the machine. Gently lower the needle until it enters the paper at the first ¼" line from the edge of the paper.

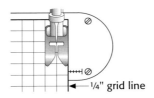

¼" grid line

2. Lower the presser foot to hold the paper in place while you apply the tape.
3. Align the tape or another marker material along the edge of the paper.

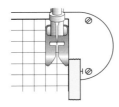

4. Lift the presser foot, raise the needle, and remove the paper. Sew a sample seam on fabric; then measure it to check for accuracy. Adjust the marker position as necessary.

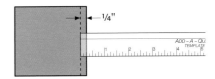

¼"

Constructing Blocks

The blocks in this book are sewn into units that are then combined to complete the quilt design. Beginning students are great at laying out the parts of each block to create the correct arrangement, but sometimes they don't understand how to place the pieces with their right sides together for sewing. Here's a way to help your students understand this concept:

1. Lay the pieces out, right sides up, to create the correct arrangement. (Each block in this book comes with illustrations that show how to arrange the pieces.)

2. Working from the left-hand side of the arrangement, imagine that pieces 1 and 2 are the covers of a book that you've just finished reading. Pick up the right-hand edge of piece 2 and bring it over piece 1 as if you were closing the book.
3. Think of the right-hand edge of the overlapped pieces as the spine of the closed book; this is where you'll sew. Draw the sewing line along this edge, pin the fabric, and sew the seam.

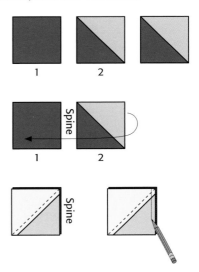

4. Press the seam in the direction indicated by the arrow in the illustration.

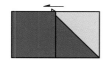

5. Place the 2 pieces, which are now joined, back in the arrangement. These pieces are now piece 1, and the piece to the right of them is the new piece 2. Close the book by bringing piece 2 over the right-hand square in piece 1. Draw the sewing line, pin, and sew. Press the seam in the direction indicated by the arrow.

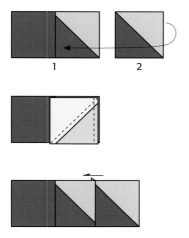

Sewing with a Machine

I learned to sew on a machine when I was nine years old, so naturally I think that's the perfect age for a beginning sewing-machine student. Let your students sew on your best machine. Remember: You want them to love sewing!

Set up a workspace in a well-lit area, and make sure each child can reach the sewing machine easily. If a child is too short to reach the foot pedal, try putting the pedal on a thick book or small box. Very small children can sew while standing up. You may be surprised by how easily they can operate sewing machines while they're standing.

Exploring the Sewing Machine

I use a three-step approach when I teach new students how to use a sewing machine. First, we set up the machine and become familiar with its parts. Next, we add power. Finally, we add thread.

Use the owner's manual with all its pictures to teach your students about the machine. Understanding how the pictures relate to the actual machine will help them feel more comfortable sewing without your supervision, which is the ultimate goal.

Children like to experiment with the sewing-machine parts to see how they work. Start by removing the bobbin and top thread and unplugging the machine, so the children can explore the machine without tangling everything in thread.

Introduce the children to the following parts of the machine:

Presser foot and lever. Point out the presser foot and the lever that raises and lowers it. Show the children how to gently lower and raise the presser foot without letting the foot slam down. Allow them to use whichever hand feels most natural.

Feed dogs. I describe the feed dogs as the bumpy teeth under the presser foot. The presser foot holds the fabric against the feed dogs, and together they move the fabric through the machine.

Needle. The needle carries the top thread down to the bobbin, where the thread loops around the bobbin thread to make a stitch. Follow the instructions in the owner's manual to change the needle. Let the children take the needle in and out several times. Make sure that a new needle is in the machine when they are ready to sew on fabric.

Take-up lever. My students have nicknamed the take-up lever the "duck's head" because on some machines, it bobs up and down like a duck. When the duck's head is up, the needle is up, and when it's down, the needle is down. When it's halfway up, so is the needle. The most important thing to teach about the take-up lever is that when the children stop sewing, the lever must be all the way up. If it isn't, when they start sewing again, the lever will rise and pull the thread out of the needle. Some machines have an automatic function that stops the lever either all the way up or all the way down. If your machine has this option, teach the children how to select the automatic-up position.

Handwheel. Point out the wheel on the right-hand side of the machine. Tell the children, "Always turn the wheel toward you. If you turn the wheel away from you, you might make a big knot." The fear of making a big knot is usually enough to teach children to turn the wheel in the right direction! Have the children watch what happens to the needle and the take-up lever as they turn the wheel with one hand: the needle and lever will move up and down in unison.

Foot pedal. Plug in the machine and attach the foot pedal. (This is a good time to talk about electrical safety.) Show the children how to turn on the machine and the light. Have the children press the foot pedal, while keeping their hands in their lap (well away from the needle). Kids often push the pedal very hard and then panic, so show them how to make the machine go slowly by using less pressure on the pedal. Also demonstrate how to stop the machine by taking your foot off the pedal. Have the children watch the parts of the machine as they run the motor, so they'll understand that pushing on the pedal makes the feed dogs go back and forth, the duck's head and needle go up and down, and the handwheel turn toward them. Show the students that the harder they push on the pedal, the faster the machine goes, and that when they let up the pressure on the pedal, the machine slows down or stops.

Stitch-length selector. Locate the stitch-length selector, and teach the children how to use it to adjust the length.

TIPS FOR SMOOTH STITCHING

Kids have a tendency to push the foot pedal away from them as they sew. If the foot pedal slides, try putting an anti-slip surface, such as a bath mat, underneath it.

If the child pushes and releases the foot pedal too abruptly, making the machine stop and start in a jerky pattern, try this: Hold the child's hand in yours, with the child's palm up. Place the fingers of your other hand in the child's palm. Tell him that your fingers are like his foot, and his hand is like the foot pedal. Now press and release your fingers against the child's palm to demonstrate how to exert continuous pressure and how to let up on the pressure gradually in order to stop the machine.

Practicing with the Sewing Machine

When the children understand all the sewing machine's parts and how they work together, have them practice sewing on lined paper, without using thread. Most presser feet have a centerline or mark. Show the children how to line up the mark with the line on the paper and how to lower the presser foot. Watch as they sew along the line and offer help as needed. When they get to the end of the line, show them how to lift the presser foot and remove the paper.

While your students are sewing on paper, assess how comfortable they are. If the foot pedal is too difficult to reach, adjust it. If they hold the paper so tightly that the feed dogs can't move it through the machine, demonstrate how to loosen the hold. Explain that the students' hands should ride along lightly on the paper as it moves under the needle.

To demonstrate stitch length, show the children how far apart the needle holes are on the practice sheet. Ask them to use the stitch-length selector to adjust the length. Have them practice sewing with different lengths, and compare the resulting stitches. Once the students understand how to adjust the stitch length, tell them that the best setting is at ten to twelve stitches per inch.

Once the children are comfortable with operating the machine and can stitch consistently along the lines on the practice paper, it's time to add thread.

Threading the Sewing Machine

Use the diagrams in the owner's manual to demonstrate threading the machine. Explain that the machine must be threaded correctly or it won't operate properly. I have my students thread the machine themselves; then they pull the thread out and do it again, following the illustrations in the owner's manual.

I tell the kids that the bobbin is just like a small spool of thread, and then I explain how the top thread loops down and catches the bobbin thread to make the stitch. The two threads work together, and if one isn't working properly, the sewing machine won't make a stitch.

Referring to the owner's manual again, teach the children how to wind the bobbin. Wind one as a sample; then have the children try. When they can wind bobbins successfully, I show them how to load the bobbin into the machine. Have students repeat this process until they're comfortable and understand what they're doing.

Chain-Piecing

The sewing in this book can be accomplished by chain-piecing—a method of feeding one set of patches right after another through the sewing machine, without cutting the threads between them. To practice, the children will need two fabric scraps and a 6" x 12" piece of muslin. Help the children through the following steps, and have them practice until they are comfortable stitching:

1. Fold the muslin in half to form a 6" x 6" square. Also fold the scraps in half. With a pencil and ruler, draw several parallel lines across the muslin, about ½" apart.

2. Place a scrap piece under the presser foot and lower the foot. Sew until the needle is almost off the fabric. Remove your foot from the foot pedal. Without lifting the presser foot, place the marked muslin almost next to the starter scrap, aligning the center mark on the presser foot with one of the lines you drew.

3. Resume sewing, letting the feed dogs grab the muslin and pull it under the presser foot and needle. Sew to the end of the line on the muslin.

4. Place another scrap in front of the feed dogs so it will feed under the needle. Sew onto this scrap. As soon as you have completely sewn off the muslin, stop sewing and cut the threads that separate the scrap and muslin.

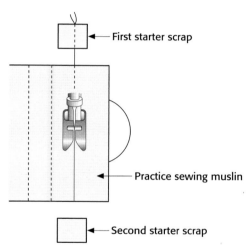

◄— First starter scrap

◄— Practice sewing muslin

◄— Second starter scrap

Making Folded Corners

Folded corners (or foldovers) have become very popular in the quilt world. Because you sew along the bias before the edges are cut, you help control stretching of the bias edges. (Kids tend to have hot little hands, which can distort the fabric!)

To make a folded corner:
1. On the wrong side of the fabric square that will become a triangle in the finished unit, draw a diagonal line from corner to corner.

2. Place the square on the corner of the base fabric, right sides together, aligning the edges carefully. Position the square so the sewing line makes a triangle at the corner. Stitch on the line.

Stitch.

3. Draw a parallel line ¼" from the stitching and trim away the corner with a rotary cutter. Press the seam toward the darker fabric unless otherwise indicated in the specific instructions.

Cut.   Press open.

USING LEFTOVERS

Each time you make a folded corner, you'll generate a pair of "waste" triangles. Don't throw them away! These leftovers are usually large enough to sew together as a nice little quilt. Create your own pattern or make small versions of some of the blocks in this book. Turn to page 4 to see two quilts made from leftover triangles.

Making Three-Step Triangle Squares

Draw, sew, and cut: These are the three steps to making the shortcut triangle squares described here. Each pair of square fabric pieces (one light and one dark) will yield two squares that are divided diagonally into triangles, often called "half-square triangles" or "bias squares." The standard measurement for the starting square is the finished size plus ⅞".

To make two triangle squares:
1. On the wrong side of the lighter-colored fabric square, draw a diagonal sewing line from corner to corner.
2. Draw 2 more lines, each parallel to the diagonal line and ¼" away from it.

3. Place the squares with their right sides together. Pin with straight pins to keep the layers from slipping.

4. Sew on the 2 outside lines; then cut along the centerline through both layers of fabric.

5. Press the seams of each triangle square toward the darker fabric, unless otherwise indicated in the specific instructions.

6. To avoid bulky seams, trim the "dog ears"—the small triangular bits of fabric that extend beyond the square's corners.

Pressing

When I'm working with children, I let them use an iron set on "cotton" without steam, and I teach them to press from the right side of the fabric. (When they press from the right side, they press fewer pleats into their patchwork.) The illustrations in this book include small arrows that point in the direction the seam should be pressed.

Show the children how to position the patchwork on the ironing board. The piece that you want the seam pressed toward should be on top. With one hand, open the patchwork enough to place the tip of the iron on the bottom piece. (Make sure the seam underneath is facing in the right direction.) Then gently open the patchwork the rest of the way while sliding the iron across the seam area. The iron will hold the piece down as it opens the patchwork.

Pressing Tips

When you're working with a first-time iron handler, have the student place his or her hand on the handle of the iron; then place your hand over the student's. You'll be in control, but the child will get a sense of what it feels like to use the iron.

When I teach children how to use an iron, I give them a few reminders.
- Always stand the iron up when you're not using it.
- Make sure nothing is touching the hot iron when it isn't in use.
- Turn the iron off when you're finished. (Some irons turn off automatically.)
- Anything you've just pressed will be hot! Let the fabric cool slightly before touching it.
- You won't burn the hand that's holding the iron, but you might burn the other one. Be aware of where that other hand is.

Children often face some common problems with pressing. Following are a few tips for handling them:

If a seam is twisted during sewing, snip into it to release the twist. Then re-press the seam until it's flat. You can also use a seam ripper to remove enough stitches to release the twisted seam; then re-sew and press again.

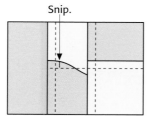

Twisted seam

Pleats are tucks that occur when a seam isn't pressed all the way open. The resulting patch will be smaller than it should be; if pleats aren't discovered and corrected, the pieces of a block may not fit together properly. Teach children to check for pleats before they join one piece to another.

It's easy to distort a piece with an iron by over-pressing. Explain to your students that when they're pressing a diagonal seam that contains bias, they should take special care to avoid pulling against the grain of the fabric. Show them how to press the length of a diagonal seam instead of across it.

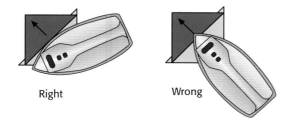

Right   Wrong

Matching Intersecting Seams

To assemble the sections of a block, first match the ends and pin them; then match and pin any intersecting seams. Finally, fill in with enough pins to keep the edges aligned.

When you're machine piecing, you'll sew the seams down in the direction they were pressed. To avoid twisting seams, you may need to pin the seam allowances.

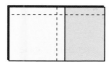

Matching two straight seams. Straight seams are most easily matched when the seams are pressed in opposite directions. The seam allowances will butt up against each other perfectly at the seam line.

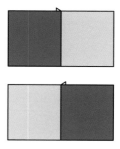

Matching a straight seam and a folded-corner seam. On the wrong side of the folded-corner piece, mark a line ¼" from the edge, as shown. From the wrong side, insert a pin where the pencil line and the stitching intersect. Looking at the right side of the straight-seam patch, insert the same pin at the seam line, ¼" from the edge. Pull the pin straight through to the wrong side of the straight-seam piece, bringing both pieces together. Pin the patches together on both sides of the first pin, and remove the first pin.

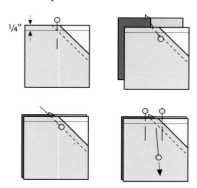

Matching two folded-corner seams. Follow the same steps as you would when matching a folded corner to a straight seam, but measure and mark the ¼" seam on the wrong sides of both patches.

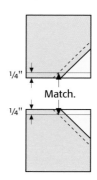

Matching two triangle seams. Usually, each triangle unit will have three intersecting lines. From the wrong side of the first piece, insert a pin where the three lines intersect. Insert the same pin through the second piece, from the right side, entering the point of the triangle. Pull the pin through to the wrong side of the second piece, bringing the two pieces together and matching the points. Pin on both sides of the first pin; then remove the first pin. If the seams are pressed so you can't see the intersecting lines, as you insert the first pin, watch from the right side for the point of the pin to come out where the seams intersect.

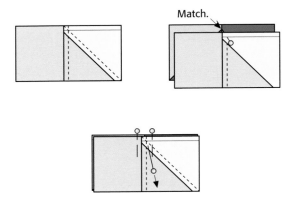

Match.

Easing

When a piece is slightly longer than it should be, you may need to ease it when you join it to another piece. In my classes, we call this process "matching the ends and squeezing the rest to fit." Show your students how to distribute the extra fabric evenly. Start by matching and pinning the two pieces at the ends and at any intersecting seams. Divide a section in half and place a pin at the center point. Subdivide each of the new sections in half, placing a pin at each center point. Continue pinning until the edges are aligned, using as many pins as necessary.

If sewing on a machine, place the fullest piece on the bottom (or bobbin side of the machine). To help your students remember this, use alliteration. Tell them, "The *big* one goes on the *bottom*."

When easing on a sewing machine, don't pull the pins out too soon or all your careful pinning efforts will be wasted. I have my students pull the pins out just before the pins feed under the presser foot.

Sometimes, whether you're easing or not, a "bubble" develops between the presser foot and the next pin. Resist the tendency to pull the pin out. Doing so will only send the fullness farther down the line to the next pin or to the end of the seam.

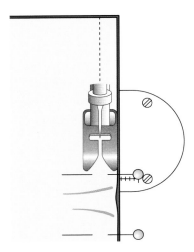

Instead of removing the pin, try this:

1. Stop sewing as soon as a bubble appears. Place one hand on the seam behind the needle, and hold the fabric there between two fingers.
2. With the index finger of your other hand, press down on the fabric in front of the needle.
3. As you continue sewing, apply gentle tension to the fabric, pulling it away from you with the hand behind the needle and toward you with the finger in front of the needle. You may have to sew across pins, as both your hands will be busy. Just sew slowly!

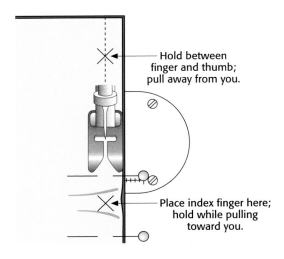

Hold between finger and thumb; pull away from you.

Place index finger here; hold while pulling toward you.

Troubleshooting Common Problems

No matter how well you teach and how serious your young stitchers are about doing great work, some of them will inevitably run into trouble along the way. Following are some of the situations that I've found to be most troublesome to my students, and the methods we use to overcome the problems:

Sewing long strip sets. Although adults are usually comfortable making long strip sets that can be cut apart into units, my experience with children is that they get bored—and sloppy—when they sew long seams.

Several blocks in this book can be made with strip sets. Feel free to adapt them to suit each child's sewing preferences. If a child is going to sew strip sets, stress the importance of maintaining accurate stitching all the way to the end of the seam. The same advice applies to long sashing strips and borders; see "Settings" (page 39) and "Borders" (page 44).

Veering off the end. When a child gets to the end of a seam, his or her stitching will sometimes veer off the end. This usually happens because of distractions. The child may be removing the last pin and putting it away, or looking for the starter scrap to end the line of stiching. Sometimes children have trouble seeing the fabric end once it moves under the presser foot. Watch the students as they sew; then explain what's happening and help them figure out ways to prevent the same error from happening again.

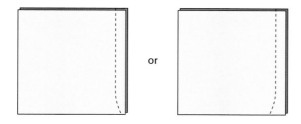

or

Uneven ends. After two pieces are sewn together and pressed, their edges should be straight and even. If a "stair-step" occurs, the next piece that's sewn won't match up properly. Resist the tendency to trim! Trimming will always catch up with you in the end. Eventually, you'll either lose the point of a triangle or end up with a piece that's too small.

Uneven ends usually occur for one of two reasons: omitting pinning altogether or taking the pins out too soon. They can also occur if you allow a bubble to progress to the end of a seam instead of easing it in. See "Easing" on page 16. To fix uneven ends, you'll need to pick out the stitches and resew the seam. Be sure to pin carefully before restitching the seam.

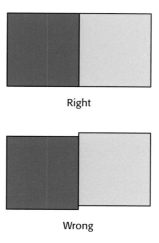

Right

Wrong

Tension problems. The tension is the tightness or looseness of the stitched thread. Each machine is adjusted differently, so refer to the owner's manual for guidance. When the tension's too tight, the seams look gathered. When it's too loose, the stitching isn't strong and will pull out easily.

Skipped stitches. If your machine is skipping stitches periodically, replace the needle.

"It was fine until I rewound the bobbin." If your machine was sewing perfectly, but suddenly started to sew improperly after you rewound the bobbin, you can safely assume that you re-threaded the machine or the bobbin casing incorrectly. Remove both the top and bobbin threads completely and re-thread them, following the instructions in the owner's manual.

"It was sewing fine at home." Whenever you move the machine for a class, make a habit of stitching a few rows before beginning on a project. It's easy to bump and change a setting when you move a machine. Discovering a problem while you work on a sample is better than discovering one during a class project.

The Block Workshop

All of the blocks in this section are fun and easy for kids to make. They're grouped by technique and can be mixed and matched for use in any of the quilt settings. For ideas, see "Settings" on pages 39–44.

MAKING BLOCK SWATCH CARDS

Make a swatch card and identify each fabric on it with the appropriate letter.

As you cut the required pieces and sort them into piles, label the piles with small pieces of paper that indicate the cut size and fabric-identification letter.

Double Nine Patch

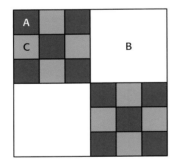

Fabric	Cut Size	No. Needed
A	2½" x 2½"	10
B	6½" x 6½"	2
C	2½" x 2½"	8

Unit 1

1. Sew a 2½" square of fabric A to 1 side of a 2½" square of fabric C, placing the right sides together and leaving a ¼" seam allowance. Repeat to sew another square of fabric A to the opposite side of the fabric C square. Press the seams toward the fabric A squares.

2. Repeat step 1 to make 3 more identical strips, pressing the seams as illustrated.

Make 4.

3. Sew 2 more strips, arranging squares of fabrics A and C as shown. Press the seams toward fabric A.

Make 2.

4. Using the illustrations as placement guides, sew 3 of the strips together. Press the seams away from the center strip. Repeat to join another 3 strips.

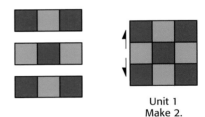

Unit 1
Make 2.

Unit 2

1. Sew a unit 1 to one side of a 6½" square of fabric B. Press the seam toward fabric B.

2. Repeat step 1 to join the other unit 1 to the other square of fabric B. Press the seam toward fabric B.

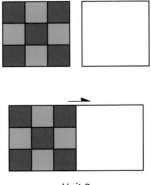

Unit 2
Make 2.

Block Assembly

Rotate one of unit 2 and sew it to the bottom of the other unit 2. Press the seam as shown in the illustration.

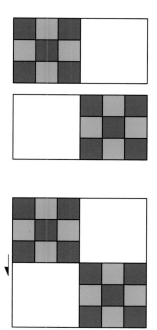

Fair and Square

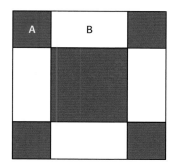

Fabric	Cut Size	No. Needed
A	6½" x 6½"	1
A	3½" x 3½"	4
B	3½" x 6½"	4

NOTE: The 6½" center square of fabric A may be cut from a different fabric than the 3½" corner squares of fabric A.

Unit 1

1. Sew a fabric B rectangle to 1 side of a 6½" square of fabric A, placing the pieces right sides together and leaving a ¼" seam allowance. Press the seam toward the fabric A square.
2. Repeat step 1 to sew another fabric B rectangle to the opposite side of the fabric A square. Press the seam toward the fabric A square.

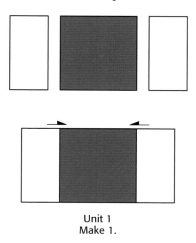

Unit 1
Make 1.

Unit 2

1. Sew a 3½" square of fabric A to one end of a rectangle of fabric B. Repeat to sew another 3½" fabric A square to the opposite end of the fabric B rectangle.
2. Press the seams toward fabric A.
3. Repeat steps 1 and 2 to join the remaining 2 fabric A squares to the other fabric B rectangle. Press the seams toward fabric A.

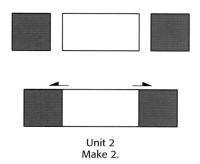

Unit 2
Make 2.

Block Assembly

1. To sew a unit 2 to the top edge of unit 1, first place the pieces right sides together. Match and pin the ends; then match and pin the seams. Insert additional pins to keep the edges aligned. Sew the pieces together, leaving a ¼" seam allowance.
2. Repeat step 1 to sew the other unit 2 to the bottom edge of unit 1.
3. Press the seams away from unit 1.

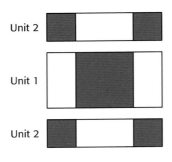

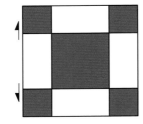

VARIATION: By making a slight change to the Fair and Square block, you can create a new block called "Monkey Wrench." Replace the 3½" corner squares of fabric A with three-step triangle squares (page 13), as shown in the illustration. To make these, cut two 3⅞" squares of fabrics A and B. The *Patch Quilt* (page 62) provides a good example of this variation.

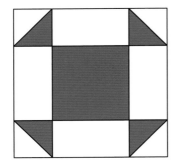

Monkey Wrench

Flag

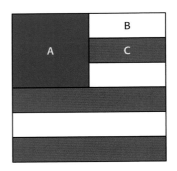

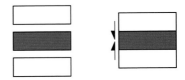

Fabric	Cut Size	No. Needed
A	6½" x 6½	1
B	2½" x 6½"	2
B	2½" x 12½"	1
C	2½" x 6½"	1
C	2½" x 12½"	2

Unit 1

1. Sew a small fabric B rectangle to a small fabric C rectangle, as shown, placing the pieces right sides together and leaving a ¼" seam allowance. Repeat to sew the other small fabric B rectangle to the opposite edge of the small fabric C rectangle.
2. Press the seams toward fabric C.
3. Sew the three-strip piece you've just made to the

right-hand side of the large square of fabric A.
4. Press the seam toward fabric A.

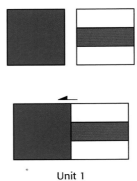

Unit 1

Unit 2

1. Sew a large fabric C rectangle to one side of the large fabric B rectangle. Repeat to sew the remaining fabric C rectangle to the opposite edge of the fabric B rectangle.
2. Press the seams toward fabric C.

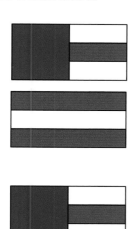

Unit 2

Block Assembly

1. To sew units 1 and 2 together, first place them with their right sides together, using the illustrations as placement guides. Pin the short ends first; then insert pins along the edges to keep the pieces aligned. Sew the units together, leaving a ¼" seam allowance.
2. Press the seam toward unit 2.

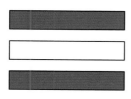

Butterfly

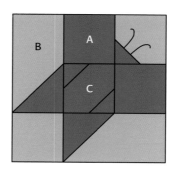

Fabric	Cut Size	No. Needed
A	4½" x 4½"	4
A	3" x 3"	2
B	4½" x 8½"	2
B	4½" x 4½"	2
C	4½" x 4½"	1
C	2½" x 2½"	1

Unit 1

1. On the wrong side of the 2½" square of fabric C, draw a diagonal line from corner to corner.

2. Using the illustrations as guides, place the fabric C square on the corner of a 4½" square of fabric B, right sides together. Align the corners and edges carefully.
3. Sew on the diagonal line. To trim the corner, cut through both layers of fabric, ¼" from the stitching. Press the seam toward fabric C.

4. Using the illustrations as placement guides, sew the section you just made (the butterfly-head section) to one side of a 4½" square of fabric A. Press the seam toward fabric A.

  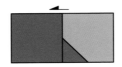

5. On the wrong side of a 3" square of fabric A, draw a diagonal line from corner to corner.

6. Using the illustrations as guides, place the fabric A square on one corner of the 4½" square of fabric C. Align the corners and edges carefully.

7. Sew on the diagonal line. Trim the corner and press the seam toward fabric C.

8. Repeat steps 5–7 to sew another 3" square of fabric A to the opposite corner of the 4½" square of fabric C. Trim the corner and press the seam toward fabric C.

9. Using the illustrations as placement guides, sew the piece you made in steps 5–8 to the edge of a 4½" square of fabric A. Press the seam toward fabric A.

  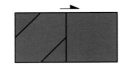

10. Sew the 2 sections together as shown. Press the seam in the direction indicated by the arrow.

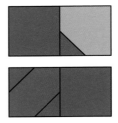 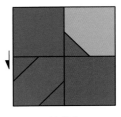

Unit 1

Units 2 and 3

1. On the wrong side of each of the 2 remaining 4½" squares of fabric A, draw a diagonal line from corner to corner.

2. Using the illustrations as guides, sew a 4½" square of fabric A to each 4½" x 8½" rectangle of fabric B. Note: These two rectangle-and-square arrangements aren't the same, so be careful when you arrange the pieces!

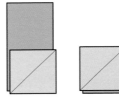

3. Sew on each diagonal line; then trim the corners. Press the seam toward fabric A on each of these units.

Unit 2a

Unit 2b

4. Using the illustrations as guides, sew a 4½" square of fabric B to one end of unit 1. Press the seam toward fabric B.

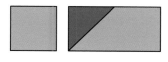

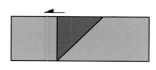

Unit 3

Block Assembly

1. Using the illustrations as guides, sew unit 2 to the left-hand side of unit 1. Press the seam toward unit 1. Ease if necessary.

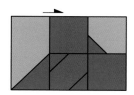

2. Referring to the illustrations again, sew unit 3 to units 1 and 2. Press the seam toward unit 3.

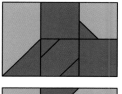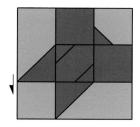

3. Draw or embroider the antennae.

House

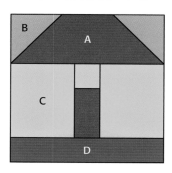

Fabric	Cut Size	No. Needed
A	4½" x 12½"	1
A	2½" x 4½"	1
B	4½" x 4½"	2
C	5½" x 6½"	2
C	2½" x 2½"	1
D	2½" x 12½"	1

Unit 1

1. On the wrong side of each 4½" square of fabric B, draw a diagonal line from corner to corner.

2. Position a fabric B square on each end of the 4½" x 12½" rectangle of fabric A, placing the right sides together. Refer to the illustrations to make sure the marked lines run in the correct directions. Sew on the diagonal lines.

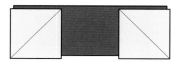

3. To trim the 2 corners, cut through both layers of fabric, ¼" from each stitching line. Press the seams toward fabric A.

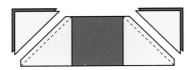

Unit 2

1. Sew the 2½" square of fabric C to an end of the 2½" x 4½" rectangle of fabric A, placing the right sides together and leaving a ¼" seam allowance. Press the seam toward fabric C.

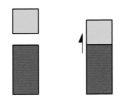

2. Sew a 5½" x 6½" rectangle of fabric C to each long side of the section you sewed in step 1. Press each seam toward a large rectangle.

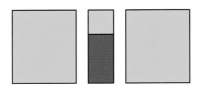

Unit 2

Block Assembly

1. Using the illustrations as guides, sew unit 1 (the roof) to the top of unit 2 (the house), easing the seam if necessary. Press the seam toward unit 2.

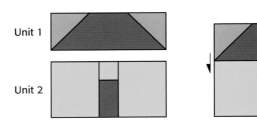

Unit 1

Unit 2

2. Sew the 2½" x 12½" strip of fabric D (it will represent grass) to the bottom of the house-and-roof section. Press the seam toward fabric D.

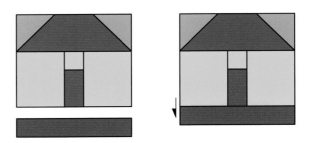

VARIATION: Instead of adding a strip of fabric D to the bottom of the house, cut a 2½" x 12½" rectangle of fabric B and stitch it above the house-and-roof section to represent the sky.

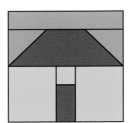

Indian Hatchet

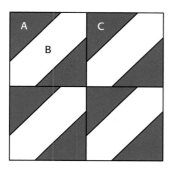

Fabric	Cut Size	No. Needed
A	4" x 4"	4
B	6½" x 6½"	4
C	4" x 4"	4

Sewing

1. Draw a diagonal sewing line from corner to corner on the wrong side of each fabric A square and each fabric C square.

2. Using the illustrations as guides, position a fabric A square on a corner of a fabric B square, placing the right sides together and aligning the edges carefully.

3. Sew on the diagonal line. To trim the corner, cut through both layers of fabric, ¼" from the stitching. Press the seam toward fabric A.

4. Repeat steps 2 and 3 to sew another fabric A square to the opposite corner of the fabric B square. Trim the corner and press the seam toward fabric B.

5. Using the remaining 2 squares of fabric A and another square of fabric B, repeat steps 2–4 to make another square just like the first one.

Make 2.

6. Repeat steps 2–5, but this time, use the 4 squares of fabric C and the 2 remaining squares of fabric B. Press the seams toward fabric C on each piece.

Make 2.

Block Assembly

1. Using the illustrations as guides, sew the sections together in pairs. Press the seams as shown.

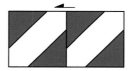

Make 2.

2. Using the illustrations as guides, rotate one section and place it on top of the other section, right sides together. Match and pin the center seam and the ends. Then sew the two pieces together, leaving a ¼" seam allowance. Press the seam as shown.

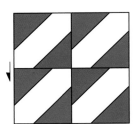

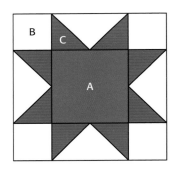

Sawtooth Star

Fabric	Cut Size	No. Needed
A	6½" x 6½"	1
B	3½" x 6½"	4
B	3½" x 3½"	4
C	3½" x 3½"	8

Unit 1

1. On the wrong side of each 3½" square of fabric C, draw a diagonal line from corner to corner.

2. Place a square of fabric C on one end of a 3½" x 6½" rectangle of fabric B, right sides together. Align the corners; then sew on the diagonal line. To trim the corner, cut through both layers of fabric, ¼" from the stitching. Press the seam toward fabric C.

3. Using the illustrations as placement guides, position another 3½" square of fabric C on the opposite end of the fabric B rectangle, right sides together. Sew on the line and trim the corner. Press the seam toward fabric C.
4. Repeat steps 2 and 3 to make three more of these "star-point" sections. Set two of them aside; you'll use them when you make unit 2.

Make 4.

5. Sew a 3½" square of fabric B to each end of one star-point section, placing the right sides together and leaving a ¼" seam allowance. Press the seams toward fabric B.
6. Repeat step 5 to attach another two 3½" squares of fabric B to another star-point section.

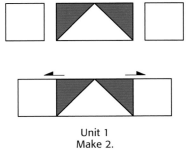

Unit 1
Make 2.

Unit 2

Sew star-point sections to opposite sides of the 6½" square of fabric A. Press the seams toward fabric A.

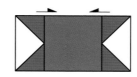

Unit 2

Block Assembly

1. Using the illustrations as guides, place a unit 1 on top of unit 2, right sides together. Match and pin the seams, easing if necessary. Sew the units together.
2. Rotate the other unit 1, and repeat step 1 to sew it to the bottom of unit 2.

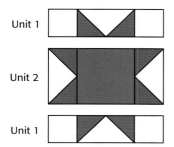

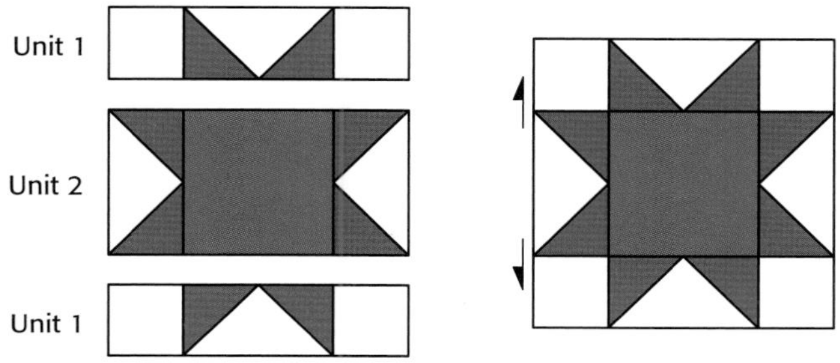

Unit 1

Unit 2

Unit 1

VARIATION: By changing the colors and rotating the star-point pieces so they point in toward the center square, you can create an entirely new block—King David's Crown. See *Patch Quilt* on page 62.

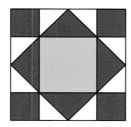

King David's Crown

Basket

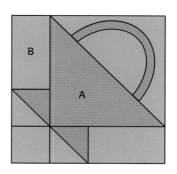

Fabric	Cut Size	No. Needed
A	10" x 13"	1
A	9⅞" x 9⅞"	1
A	3⅞" x 3⅞"	1
B	9⅞" x 9⅞"	1
B	3⅞" x 3⅞"	1
B	3½" x 3½"	1
B	3½" x 6½"	2

Unit 1

1. To cut the 1½" x 12" bias strip for the handle, first take a look at the cutting illustrations. Then align the 45° line on your ruler with the cut edge of the 10" x 13" rectangle of fabric A, as shown. Mark and cut out the strip.

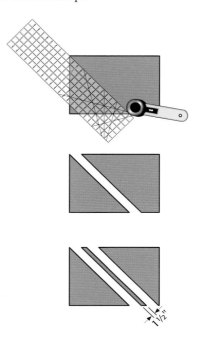

2. Cut the 9⅞" squares of fabrics A and B in half diagonally to make 4 triangles. (You'll only need 1 triangle of each fabric for each block you make; set the other 2 aside.)

3. Make a copy of the pattern on page 30 to use as a template for the handle. Mark the centerline on your copy, and then cut it out.

4. To find the center of the fabric A triangle that you cut in step 1, first fold it in half. Crease the fabric to mark the centerline; then unfold the triangle.

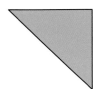

5. Place the handle pattern on the fabric B triangle, matching the centerline on the pattern with the fold in the fabric and aligning the pattern with the triangle's bottom edge. Use chalk to mark the pattern outline on the fabric. Remove the pattern.

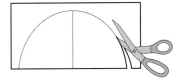

6. Fold the bias strip in half along its length, and press it. (Be careful to avoid stretching the fabric.)

7. Using plenty of straight pins, pin the folded bias strip to the triangle, aligning the strip's raw edges with the chalk line. Refer to the illustrations to make sure you position the bias strip correctly.

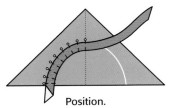

Position.

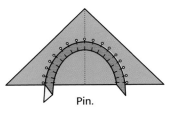

Pin.

8. Sew along the raw edge of the folded bias strip, leaving a ¼" seam allowance.

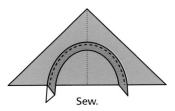

Sew.

9. Flip the folded edge of the strip over the stitching; it should cover the cut edges of the strip. Press the strip, and pin it in place so it lies flat and smooth. Using matching thread, either machine stitch very close to the folded edge or use a blind stitch (page 75) to appliqué the handle in place. For a smooth finish, press the strip again.

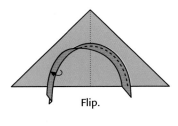

Flip.

Machine stitch or blindstitch.

10. Place the "handle" triangle on a fabric A triangle, with their right sides together. Match the ends first; then align the long edges and pin them. Sew along the edge, leaving a ¼" seam allowance. If you're sewing with a machine, position the patch with the fabric B triangle on the bottom.
11. Press the seam toward fabric A. Trim the dog ears.

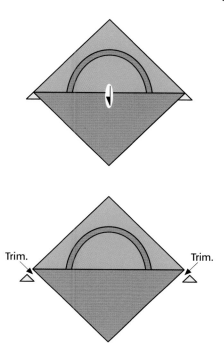

 Trim.   Trim.

Unit 1

Units 2a and 2b

1. On the wrong side of the 3⅞" square of fabric B, draw a diagonal line from corner to corner.
2. Draw 2 more lines, each parallel to and ¼" from the first line.

3. Place the fabric B square on top of the 3⅞" square of fabric A, right sides together. Sew on the 2 outside lines; then cut along the centerline through both layers of fabric.

4. Press the seam of each triangle toward fabric A. Trim the dog ears.

5. Using the illustrations as placement guides, sew a triangle square to an end of each 3½" x 6½" rectangle of fabric B, placing the right sides together and leaving ¼" seam allowances. (Be careful: These two arrangements aren't identical!) Press the seams toward the rectangles.

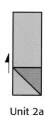

Unit 2a   Unit 2b

Block Assembly

1. Using the illustrations as guides, sew unit 2a to the left-hand side of unit 1. Press the seam toward unit 1.

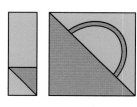 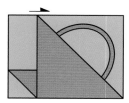

Unit 2a   Unit 1

2. Using the illustrations as guides, sew the 3½" square of fabric B to unit 2b. Press the seam toward the fabric B square.

Unit 2b

3. Sew unit 2b to the bottom of unit 1 as shown.
   Press the seam toward unit 2b.

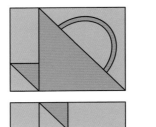 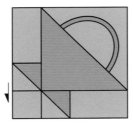

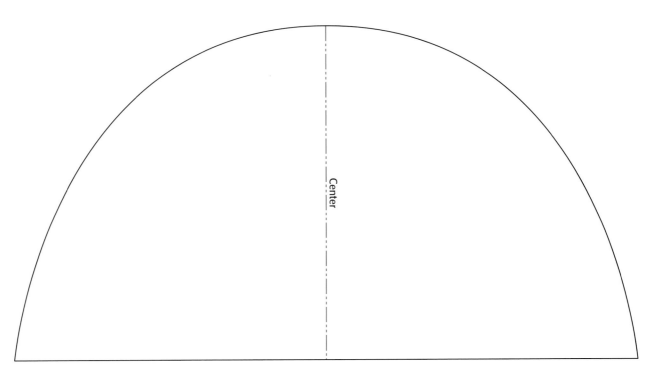

Basket Handle Pattern

Friendship Star

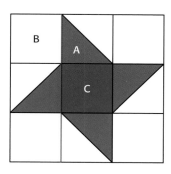

Fabric	Cut Size	No. Needed
A	4⅞" x 4⅞"	2
B	4⅞" x 4⅞"	2
B	4½" x 4½"	4
C	4½" x 4½"	1

Unit 1

1. Refer to "Making Three-Step Triangle Squares" on page 13. On the wrong side of each 4⅞" square of fabric B, draw a diagonal line from corner to corner. Draw 2 more lines on each square, parallel to and ¼" from the first line.
2. Position a square of fabric B on top of a square of fabric A, with their right sides together. Sew on the two outside lines; then cut along the centerline through both layers of fabric. Press the seam on each piece toward fabric A. Trim the dog ears.
3. Repeat step 2 with the other 4⅞" square of fabric B and the remaining square of fabric A.
4. Using the illustrations as guides, sew two 4½" squares of fabric B to a triangle square, placing the right sides together and leaving ¼" seam allowances. Press the seams toward fabric B.
5. Repeat step 4 with 2 more 4½" squares of fabric B and 1 more triangle square.

   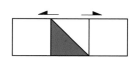

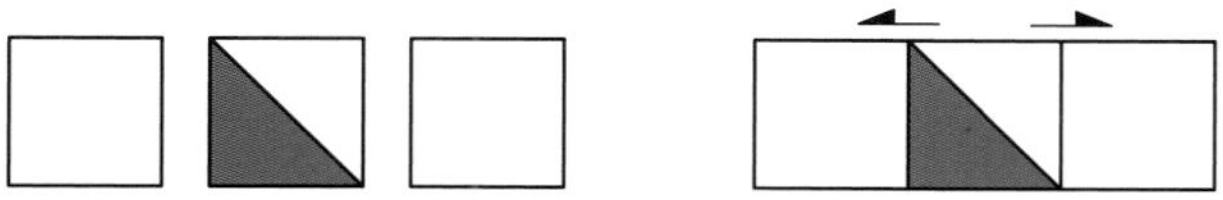

Unit 1
Make 2.

Unit 2

Sew the remaining 2 triangle squares to the ends of the 4½" square of fabric C, as shown. Press the seams toward fabric C.

   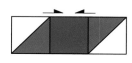

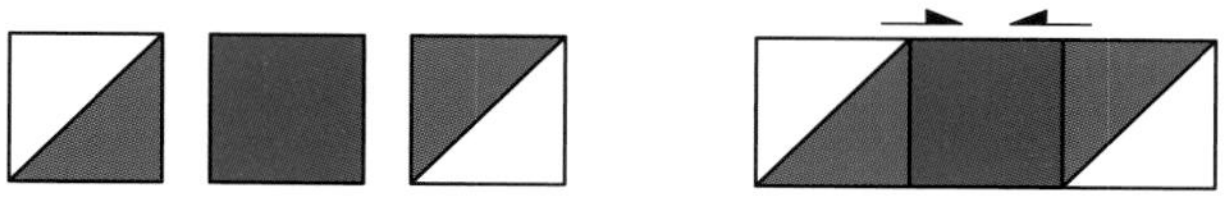

Unit 2
Make 1.

Block Assembly

1. Arrange the rows as illustrated, with a unit 1 at the top, unit 2 in the center, and the other unit 1 rotated and placed on the bottom. Be careful to arrange the units correctly. In *Cousins by the Row* (page 55), the stars "spin" in the opposite direction; the triangle squares in each unit were positioned in a different manner.
2. Place the upper unit 1 on unit 2, right sides together. Match and pin the seams; then pin the ends, using enough pins to keep the edges aligned. Sew the units together and press the seam toward unit 1.
3. Repeat step 2 to attach the other unit 1 to the bottom of unit 2. Press the seam toward unit 2.

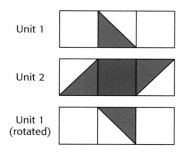

Unit 1

Unit 2

Unit 1 (rotated)

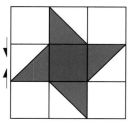

Pinwheel

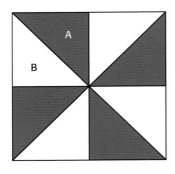

Fabric	Cut Size	No. Needed
A	6⅞" x 6⅞"	2
B	6⅞" x 6⅞"	2

Sewing

1. On the wrong side of each square of the lightest fabric, draw a diagonal line from corner to corner. Draw 2 more lines on each of these squares, parallel to and ¼" from the first line.
2. Place a light square on top of a dark square, right sides together. Sew on the two outside lines. Cut along the centerline through both layers of fabric. Press the seam toward the darker fabric. Trim the dog ears.
3. Repeat step 2 with the other fabric A square and fabric B square.

Block Assembly

1. Using the illustrations as guides, sew 1 triangle square to another, placing their right sides together and leaving a ¼" seam allowance. Pay special attention to matching the points of the triangles. (See "Matching Intersecting Seams" on page 15.) Press the seam toward the darker fabric.
2. Repeat step 1 to sew the other 2 triangle squares together.

  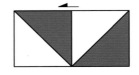

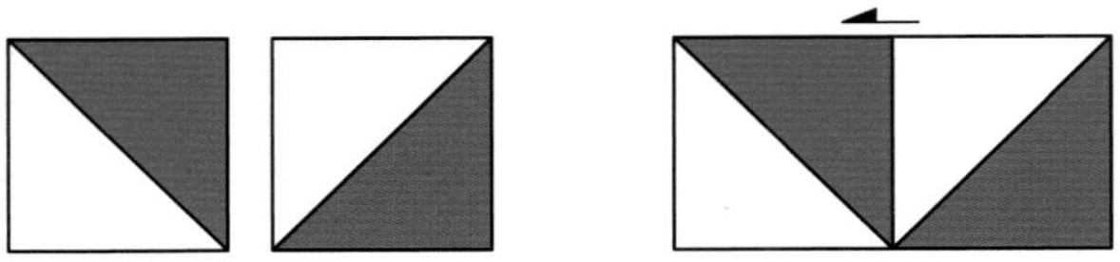

Make 2.

3. Rotate one of the pairs and arrange it with the other pair to create a pinwheel, as shown. Match and pin the center seam; then pin the ends, using enough pins to keep the edges aligned. Sew the pieces together. Press the seam as shown.

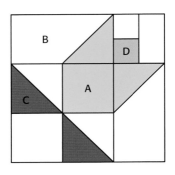

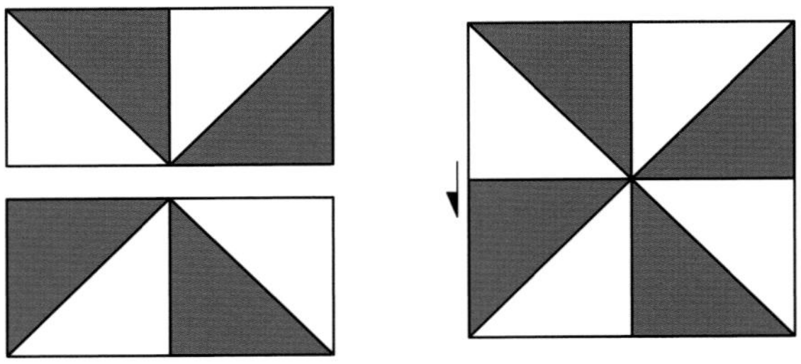

Flower

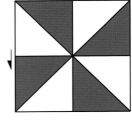

Fabric	Cut Size	No. Needed
A	4½" x 4½"	3
B	4⅞" x 4⅞"	1
B	4½" x 4½"	1
B	4½" x 8½"	2
B	2½" x 4½"	1
B	2½" x 2½"	1
C	4⅞" x 4⅞"	1
D	2½" x 2½"	1

Units 1a and 1b

1. On the wrong sides of two 4½" squares of fabric A, draw diagonal sewing lines from corner to corner.
2. Using the illustrations as guides, place 1 fabric A square on each 4½" x 8½" rectangle of fabric B, with their right sides together. Note: Each of these pairs is arranged in a different way.

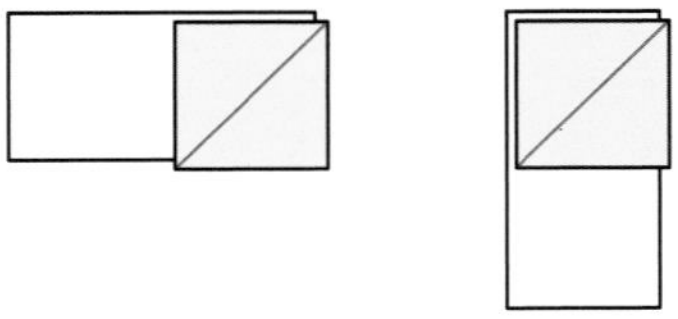

3. Sew the pairs on the diagonal lines.
4. To trim the corners, cut through both layers of fabric, ¼" from each stitched line, as shown. Press the seams toward fabric A.

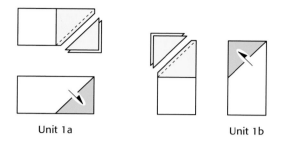

Unit 1a   Unit 1b

Unit 2

1. Sew the 2½" square of fabric D to the 2½" square of fabric B, placing their right sides together and leaving a ¼" seam allowance. Press the seam toward fabric D.

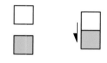

2. Using the illustrations as guides, sew the 2½" x 4½" rectangle of fabric B to the piece you sewed in step 1. Press the seam toward the rectangle.

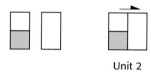

Unit 2

Unit 3

1. Refer to "Making Three-Step Triangle Squares" on page 13. On the wrong side of the 4⅞" square of fabric B, draw a diagonal line from corner to corner. Draw 2 more lines, each parallel to and ¼" from the first line.
2. Place the fabric B square on the 4⅞" square of fabric C. Sew on the two outside lines. Cut along the centerline through both layers of fabric. Press the seam toward fabric C. Trim the dog ears.
3. Using the illustrations as guides, sew the 4½" square of fabric B to one of the triangle squares you made in step 2. (Make sure you position these squares correctly.) Press the seam toward fabric B.

4. Using the illustrations as guides, sew the other triangle square to a 4½" square of fabric A. Press the seam toward fabric A.

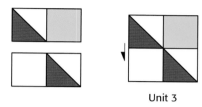

5. Sew the two sections together as illustrated, carefully matching the points on each one. Press the seam as shown.

Unit 3

Block Assembly

1. Take a good look at the illustrations; then sew unit 2 to unit 1a. (Make sure that you're using the correct unit 1.) Press the seam toward unit 2.

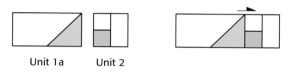

Unit 1a   Unit 2

2. Sew unit 1b to one side of unit 3, as shown. Press the seam toward unit 3.

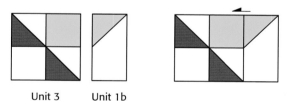

Unit 3   Unit 1b

3. Sew the 2 sections together as shown, matching and pinning the seams and ends first. Press the seam in the direction shown.

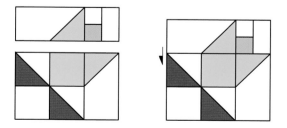

Leaf

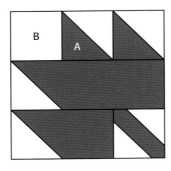

Fabric	Cut Size	No. Needed
A	4⅞" x 4⅞"	1
A	4½" x 12½"	1
A	4½" x 8½"	1
A	4½" x 4½"	1
B	4⅞" x 4⅞"	1
B	4½" x 4½"	3
B	4" x 4"	2

Unit 1

1. On the wrong side of the 4⅞" square of fabric B, draw a diagonal line from corner to corner. Draw 2 more lines, each parallel to and ¼" from the first line.
2. Place the 4⅞" square of fabric B on the 4⅞" square of fabric A, with their right sides together. Sew on the 2 outside lines. Cut along the centerline through both layers of fabric.
3. Press the seams toward the darker fabric. Trim the dog ears.
4. Using the illustrations as guides, arrange a 4½" square of fabric B and the 2 triangle squares that you just made. Sew the 3 pieces together, leaving ¼" seam allowances. Press the seams toward the fabric B square.

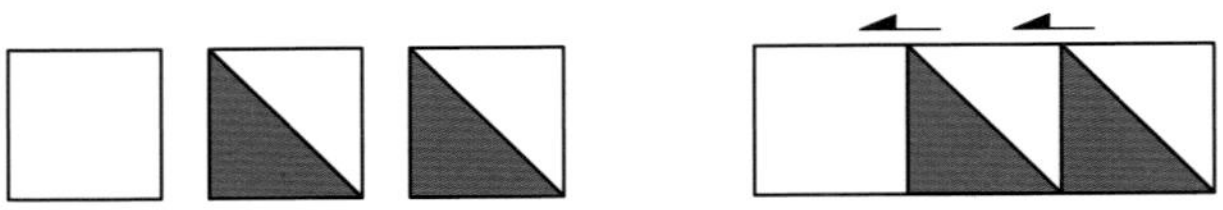

Unit 1

Unit 2

1. On each of the remaining two 4½" squares of fabric B, draw a diagonal sewing line from corner to corner.
2. Place 1 of these fabric B squares on the end of the 4½" x 12½" rectangle of fabric A. (Set aside the other 4½" square of fabric B.) Carefully align the corners and refer to the illustrations to make sure the sewing line runs in the correct direction. Sew on the line.

3. To trim the corner, cut through both layers of fabric, ¼" from the stitching. Press the seam toward fabric A.

Unit 2

Unit 3

1. On the wrong side of each 4" square of fabric B, draw a sewing line from corner to corner.
2. Place one 4" fabric B square on the 4½" square of fabric A, with their right sides together. Carefully align the corners. Sew on the line.

3. To trim the corner, cut through both layers of fabric, ¼" from the stitching. Press the seam toward fabric A.

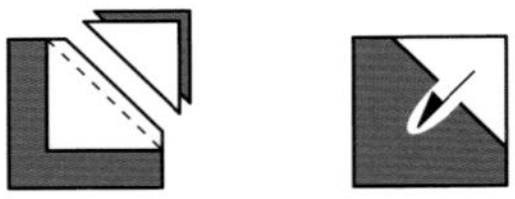

4. Place the other 4" square of fabric B on the opposite corner of the 4½" square of fabric A. Refer to the illustrations to make sure you position the sewing line correctly. Sew on the line.
5. Trim the corner and press the seam toward fabric A.

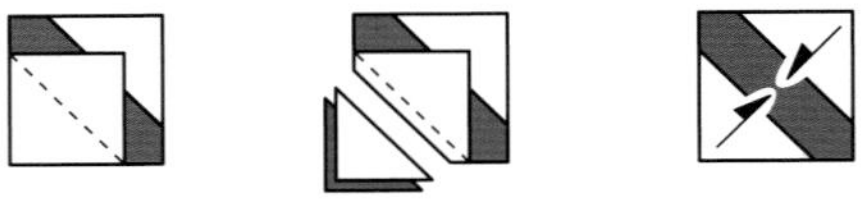

6. Place the remaining 4½" square of fabric B on the end of the 4½" x 8½" rectangle of fabric A, with their right sides together, referring to the illustrations for correct placement. Carefully align the corners. Sew on the line.

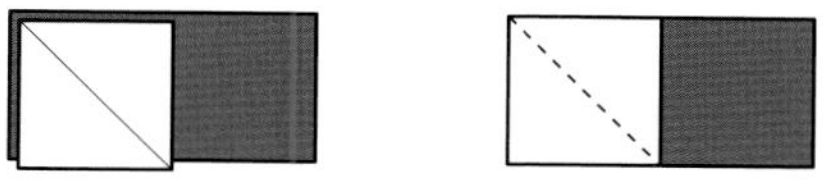

7. Trim the corner and press the seam toward fabric A.

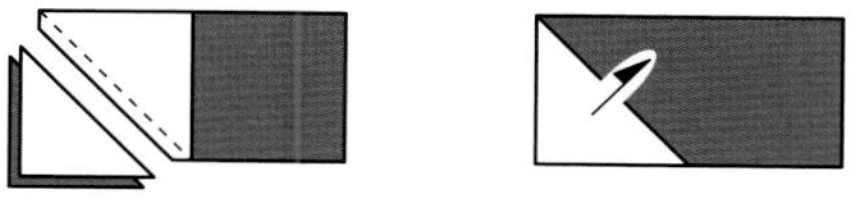

8. To complete unit 3, sew the "stem" piece to the end of the section you just made. Be sure the stem is pointing the right direction! Press the seam away from the stem.

 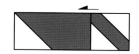

Unit 3

Block Assembly

1. Compare unit 2 and unit 1. If unit 2 is too long, trim it as shown in the illustration.

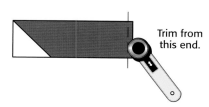

Trim from this end.

2. Join units 1, 2, and 3, placing the right sides together, matching the seams and ends, and leaving ¼" seam allowances. If necessary, ease to fit. (See "Easing" on page 16.) Press both seams toward unit.

Unit 1
Unit 2
Unit 3

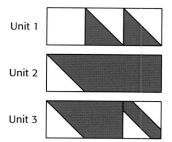 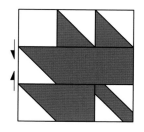

Pine Tree

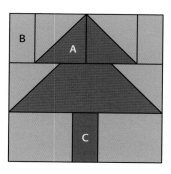

Fabric	Cut Size	No. Needed
A	4⅞" x 4⅞"	1
A	4½" x 12½"	1
B	4⅞" x 4⅞"	1
B	4½" x 4½"	2
B	2½" x 4½"	2
B	4½" x 5½"	2
C	2½" x 4½"	1

Unit 1

1. Refer to "Making Three-Step Triangle Squares" on page 13. On the wrong side of the 4⅞" square of fabric B, draw a diagonal line from corner to corner. Draw 2 more lines, each parallel to and ¼" from the first line.

2. Place the 4⅞" square of fabric A on the 4⅞" square of fabric B, with their right sides together. Sew on the 2 outside lines. Then cut along the centerline through both layers of fabric. Press the seams toward fabric A on 1 of the triangle squares and toward fabric B on the other.

3. To make the treetop, sew the 2 triangle squares together, as shown, carefully matching the points in the center and leaving a ¼" seam allowance. Press the seam as shown.

4. Sew a 2½" x 4½" rectangle of fabric B to each side of the treetop section. Press the seams toward the rectangles.

Unit 1

Unit 2

1. On the wrong side of each 4½" square of fabric B, draw a diagonal line from corner to corner.
2. Using the illustrations as guides, place one 4½" fabric B square on each end of the 4½" x 12½" rectangle of fabric A, right sides together. Sew on the lines. To remove the corners, cut through both layers of fabric, ¼" from the stitching lines. Press the seams toward fabric A.

Unit 2

Unit 3

Sew a 4½" x 5½" rectangle of fabric B to each side of the 2½" x 4½" rectangle of fabric C. Press the seams toward fabric C.

Unit 3

Block Assembly

1. Pin and sew unit 1 to unit 2, matching the ends and easing to fit if necessary. Press the seam toward unit 2.
2. Pin and sew unit 3 to the bottom of unit 2. Press the seam toward unit 3.

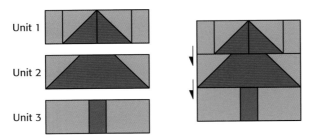

Unit 1
Unit 2
Unit 3

VARIATION: If you want to arrange the blocks in rows, as in the *Ranger's Cabin* quilt (page 66), alternate the direction of the seams in the final pressing step so that half of the blocks are pressed as shown, and the other half are pressed with the seams facing away from unit 3.

Railroad Crossing

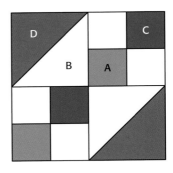

Fabric	Cut Size	No. Needed
A	3½" x 3½"	2
B	6⅞" x 6⅞"	1
B	3½" x 3½"	4
C	3½" x 3½"	2
D	6⅞" x 6⅞"	1

Unit 1

1. On the wrong side of the 6⅞" square of fabric B, draw a diagonal line from corner to corner. Draw 2 more lines, each parallel to and ¼" from the first line.
2. Place the 6⅞" square of fabric B on the 6⅞" square of fabric D, with their right sides together. Sew on the 2 outside lines. Then cut along the centerline through both layers of fabric. Press each seam toward fabric D. Trim the dog ears.

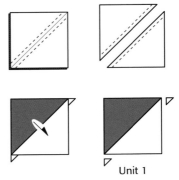

Unit 1

Unit 2

1. Sew a 3½" square of fabric B to a 3½" square of fabric C, placing them right sides together and leaving a ¼" seam allowance. Press the seam toward fabric C.
2. Repeat step 1 to sew another 3½" square of fabric B to another 3½" square of fabric C. Press the seam toward fabric C.

Make 2.

3. Sew a 3½" square of fabric A to a 3½" square of fabric B. Press the seam toward fabric A.
4. Repeat to join another 3½" fabric A square and another 3½" fabric B square. Press the seam toward fabric A.

Make 2.

5. Sew together 2 of the pairs you've just made. Press the seam as shown in the illustration.

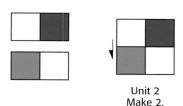

Unit 2
Make 2.

6. Repeat step 5 to sew the remaining 2 pairs together.

Block Assembly

1. Sew one unit 1 and one unit 2 together, as shown. (Because unit 2 has 3 different fabrics, identical fabrics won't always end up right next to each other when you set the units side by side.) Press the seam toward unit 2.

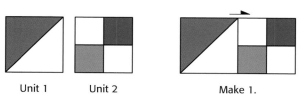

Unit 1   Unit 2   Make 1.

2. Again referring to the illustrations, sew the other unit 1 and unit 2 together. Press the seam toward unit 2.

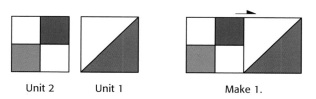

Unit 2   Unit 1   Make 1.

3. Using the illustrations as guides, place the 2 pairs right sides together, match the center seam and ends, and pin. Use enough pins to keep the edges aligned. Sew the pairs together, leaving a ¼" seam allowance. Press the seam as shown.

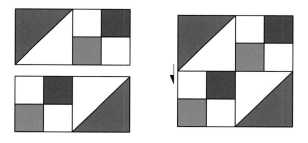

Sailboat

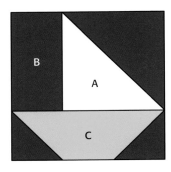

Fabric	Cut Size	No. Needed
A	8⅞" x 8⅞"	1
B	8⅞" x 8⅞"	1
B	4½" x 8½"	1
B	4½" x 4½"	2
C	4½" x 12½"	1

Unit 1

1. Refer to "Making Three-Step Triangle Squares" on page 13. On the wrong side of the 8⅞" square of fabric B, draw a diagonal line from corner to corner. Draw 2 more lines, each parallel to and ¼" from the first line.
2. Place the 8⅞" square of fabric B on the 8⅞" square of fabric A, with their right sides together.
3. Sew on the two outside lines. Cut along the centerline through both layers of fabric.
4. Press each seam toward fabric B. Trim the dog ears. (You'll only need 1 of these triangle squares for each block, so set the other aside.)
5. Sew the 4½" x 8½" rectangle of fabric B to the left side of 1 of the triangle units you've just made, placing the right sides together and leaving a ¼" seam allowance. Press the seam toward the rectangle.

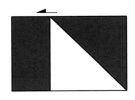

Unit 1

Unit 2

1. On the wrong side of each 4½" square of fabric B, draw a diagonal line from corner to corner.
2. Using the illustration as a guide, place one of these 4½" squares of fabric B on each end of the 4½" x 12½" rectangle of fabric C, with their right sides together.

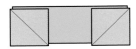

3. Sew on the diagonal lines. To remove the corners, cut through both layers of fabric, ¼" from each stitched line. Press each seam toward fabric C.

Unit 2

Block Assembly

Referring to the illustrations, place unit 1 on top of unit 2, right sides together. Match the ends, and pin. Sew the pieces together with a ¼" seam allowance, easing if necessary. Press the seam toward unit 2.

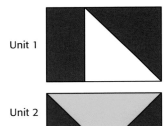
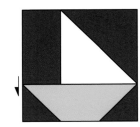

Unit 1

Unit 2

Settings

 In this section, you'll find basic instructions for four different quilt-block settings (or arrangements of pieced quilt blocks). Some of these settings include sashing strips of fabric that separate the blocks within a quilt. One also includes cornerstones, which are small squares placed at the intersections of the sashing strips. A child can create his own unique quilt both by mixing and matching the blocks in it, and by using the setting of his choice.

Sashings without Cornerstones

SAMPLE QUILTS:
Blue Sampler (page 49), *Fall Leaves* (page 54), and *Sarah's Sampler* (page 69)

This setting is a good choice for a sampler quilt or for a quilt made with many fabrics. It's a "quiet" setting—one that lets the individual blocks make their own visual statements.

Using this setting sometimes results in stair steps (misaligned blocks and sashing strips). For neatly aligned rows, pay careful attention to steps 5–7 in the instructions that follow.

Some of the sashing strips run across the quilt in this setting, and others run vertically. If you're using a directional print for your sashings, such as a stripe or a pictorial print, before you cut your fabric, take a look at the illustration for cutting directional fabrics. By cutting some strips horizontally and others vertically, you'll be able to arrange the strips in your setting so their designs will run in the same direction.

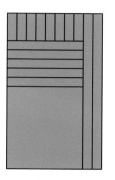
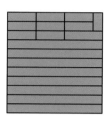

Cutting plan for
non-directional fabrics

Cutting plan for
directional fabrics

1. Cut the required number of sashing strips, using the information provided in the chart that accompanies your selected quilt plan. Remember to take directional fabrics into consideration as you do this. From the long strips that you cut, first cut the short, vertical strips that will go between the blocks. Then, leaving ¼" seam allowances, sew the ends of the remaining strips together to make 1 long strip. Press the seams open.

2. Sew the blocks and short, vertical sashing strips together to make each horizontal row for your quilt, leaving ¼" seam allowances. Press the seams toward the sashing strips.

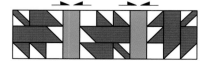

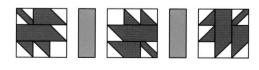

Sew blocks into rows.

3. Measure the length of each row and calculate an average row length. From the long strip, cut 1 horizontal sashing strip to this length for each row. Also cut 1 extra horizontal strip from the long strip; you'll add this strip to the top of the first row of blocks. (If the border fabric for your quilt is different from the sashing fabric, cut 2 of these horizontal strips from the border fabric instead of from the sashing fabric. These 2 strips will serve as the top and bottom borders of your quilt.)

4. Match and pin the center point and ends of each sashing strip to the center point and ends at the bottom of each row of blocks, easing if necessary. Sew each strip to a row, leaving a ¼" seam allowance. Press the seams toward the sashing strips.

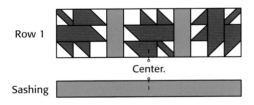

Center.

Sashing

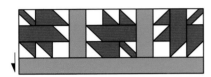

5. Place a row of sewn blocks and strips on your work surface, right side down. Align a ruler with the stitching line of a vertical strip, letting the ruler extend over the horizontal strip beneath it. Mark the edge of the horizontal strip, as shown in the illustration. Continue until you've marked every stitching line on the horizontal strip.

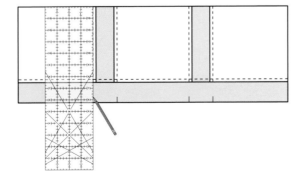

6. Place the next row of sewn blocks and strips on the marked row, right sides together, aligning the marks you made on the horizontal sashing strip with the seams of the vertical strips in the second row. Pin at each mark and at the ends, using enough pins to align the edges. Sew the new row in place, leaving a ¼" seam allowance, and press the seam toward the horizontal sashing strip.

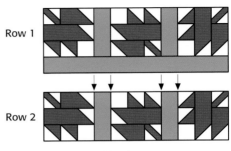

Row 1

Row 2

Match seams.

7. Repeat steps 5 and 6 to mark and sew the remaining rows. Then sew a horizontal sashing strip to the top of the quilt, matching and pinning the center point and ends, and easing if necessary. Press the seams toward the sashing strips. (If the borders of your quilt are cut from a different fabric than the sashing strips, remember to attach border fabric instead of sashing fabric.)

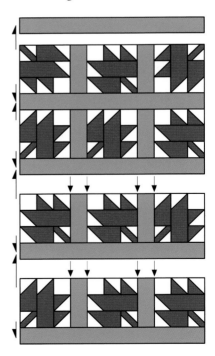

8. Measure the sewn rows from top to bottom, in the center of the quilt. Cut 2 vertical sashing strips to this length. (If your border fabric is different from your sashing fabric, cut these 2 strips from the border fabric.)

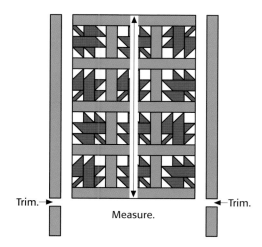

Trim.→   ←Trim.

Measure.

9. Match and pin the center point and ends of the vertical sashing (or border) strips and the vertical edges of the quilt, using enough pins to keep the edges aligned and easing if necessary. Sew the strips to the quilt, leaving ¼" seam allowances. Press the seams toward the vertical strips.

Sashings with Cornerstones

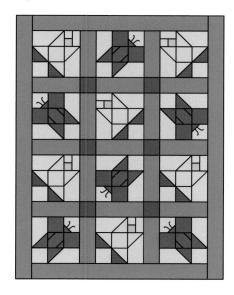

SAMPLE QUILTS:
Butterflies II (page 52) and
Patch Quilt (page 62)

In this setting, the blocks and sashing are arranged in rows that include cornerstones (small squares placed at the intersections of the sashing strips). Although cutting and sewing the pieces for a setting with cornerstones takes time, sewing the rows together is relatively easy, as the cornerstones provide ready-made matching points along each row.

Before cutting the strips and squares, refer to the cutting illustrations on page 39. If you're using directional prints, remember that some of the sashing strips in your quilt will run vertically and others horizontally, so cut the strips accordingly.

1. Cut the required number of sashing strips and cornerstones, using the information provided in the chart that accompanies your selected quilt plan.

2. Sew the blocks and vertical sashing strips together to make each horizontal row for your quilt, using ¼" seam allowances. Press the seams toward the sashing strips.

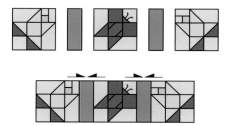

3. Sew each row of horizontal sashing strips and cornerstones, placing the pieces right sides together and using ¼" seam allowances. Press the seams toward the strips.

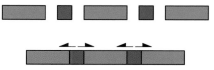

4. Sew a sashing-with-cornerstones strip to the bottom of each row of blocks, omitting the bottom row. Press the seams toward the sashing-with-cornerstones strips.

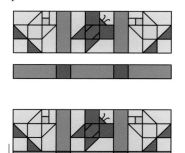

5. To sew the horizontal rows together, start by placing one row on top of another, right sides together. Align the seams carefully. Pin at each seam and at the ends, using enough pins to align the edges. Sew the two rows together, leaving a ¼" seam allowance, and press the seam toward the sashing-with-corner-stones strip. Repeat to add the other rows.

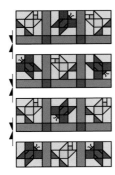

6. To complete the quilt top, follow the instructions provided in "Borders" on page 44.

Next to Each Other

SAMPLE QUILTS:
BECKY'S STARS (PAGE 46) AND *IRISH CHAIN* (PAGE 59)
This setting is appropriate for designs with repeat blocks of the same pattern or alternating blocks of two or more different patterns. It's most successful when the main design components of each block are arranged on a diagonal (this creates a chain effect), or when the corners of the blocks differ in shape or color. (Blocks with corners that are the same shape or color tend to blur together visually when the blocks are arranged side by side.)

When identical blocks are set next to each other in your quilt, you'll need to consider the directions in which the seam allowances are pressed. Ideally, the seams that meet should be pressed in opposite directions, so that matching them will be easier and more successful. See "Matching Intersecting Seams" on page 15. Spend some time studying the pressing directions and making any changes before you begin block construction.

1. Arrange the blocks according to your quilt plan. Number the rows from top to bottom by pinning a small piece of paper to a block in each row. Then sew the blocks together to make each horizontal row, using ¼" seam allowances. Press the seams to the left in even-numbered rows and to the right in odd-numbered rows.

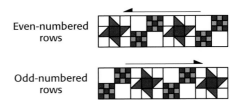

Even-numbered rows

Odd-numbered rows

2. Pin rows 1 and 2 together, right sides together, matching and pinning the ends and each seam where the blocks meet. (Butting the seams against each other will be easier if the seam allowances have been pressed in opposite directions.) Also match and pin any other seams that meet. Use enough pins to keep the edges aligned.
3. Sew the 2 rows together, leaving a ¼" seam allowance. Press the seam toward the bottom of the quilt.
4. Repeat step 3 to add the remaining rows.

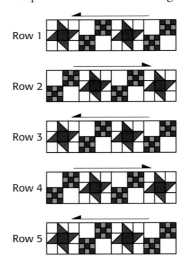

Row 1

Row 2

Row 3

Row 4

Row 5

5. To complete the quilt top, follow the instructions provided in "Borders" on page 44.

Row by Row

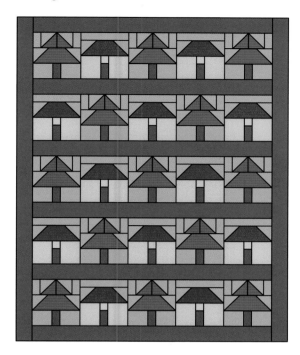

SAMPLE QUILTS:
COUSINS BY THE ROW (PAGE 55) AND
RANGER'S CABIN (PAGE 66)

In this setting, horizontal sashing strips separate rows of blocks that are arranged next to each other, and outer borders frame the quilt. (All of the quilts in this book feature rows that run horizontally across the quilt.) A variation on this setting is to arrange the rows of blocks vertically.

For this setting, as for the Next to Each Other setting, select blocks that have different shapes or colors in their corners, so the blocks won't blur together visually when they're joined. Consider changing the color placement. The House block (page 23) can be used successfully in a row if the blocks alternate grass and sky. (Alternating these strips will make the blocks look as if they're arranged in a staggered line.) Study the block patterns to find ways to customize them for a row-by-row setting.

1. Sew the blocks together to make each horizontal row for your quilt, leaving ¼" seam allowances. Press the seams to either side.

2. Measure the length of each row and calculate the average length. Using this average length and the information provided in the chart that accompanies your selected quilt plan, cut the required number of horizontal sashing strips. (You may need to sew 2 sashing strips together to make a strip that's long enough.) Press the seams open.

3. Position a horizontal sashing strip at the bottom of each row, omitting the bottom row. Match and pin the center point and ends of each sashing strip to the center point and ends at the bottom of each row of blocks, easing if necessary. Use enough pins to keep the edges aligned. Sew each strip to its row, using a ¼" seam allowance. Press the seams toward the sashing strips.

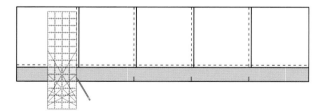

4. Place a row of sewn blocks on your work surface, right side down. Align a ruler with the stitching where 2 blocks connect, and let the ruler extend over the horizontal sashing strip beneath. Mark the edge of the horizontal sashing strip, as shown in the illustration. Repeat to mark the sashing strip at each seam where a block is connected to another block.

5. Place the next row of sewn blocks on the marked row, right sides together, aligning the seams of connecting blocks with the marks you made in step 4. Pin at each mark and at the ends, using enough pins to align the edges and easing if necessary. Sew the new row in place, using a ¼" seam allowance, and press the seam toward the sashing strip.

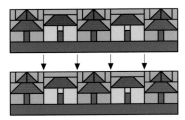

Match seams.

6. Repeat steps 4 and 5 to mark and stitch the remaining rows.

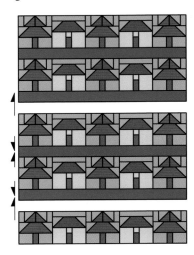

7. To complete the quilt top, see "Borders" below.

Borders

 Borders are the strips of fabric used to frame a quilt. Sewing custom-fitted borders is the final step to making a quilt that will lie or hang flat and straight. Although it's tempting to cut the borders and sew them on without measuring or pinning, if you do, the edges of your quilt may ripple!

1. Referring to the cutting information that accompanies your selected quilt plan, cut the required number of border strips. Sew their short ends together, leaving ¼" seam allowances, to make 1 long strip. Press the seams open.

2. Measure across the quilt, through its center. From the long strip you made in step 1, cut 2 horizontal border strips to this length.

Measure across the quilt and cut
top and bottom borders this length.

3. Place 1 strip at the top of the quilt, right sides together. Match and pin the strip's center point and ends with the center point and ends of the quilt, easing if necessary and using enough pins to keep the edges aligned. Sew the strip to the quilt, using a ¼" seam allowance. Press the seam toward the border. Repeat to add the bottom border strip.

4. Measure the quilt through the center, from top to bottom, including the top and bottom borders. Cut 2 vertical border strips to this length.

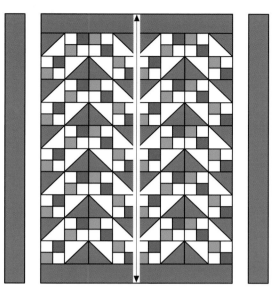

Measure the length of the quilt and
cut side borders this length.

5. Match, pin, and sew the strips to the quilt, just as you did in step 3, using ¼" seam allowances. Press the seams toward the borders.

Becky's Stars

Becky's Stars made by Becky Martin, age 14, 2000, with help from her aunt, Carol Martin, Willows, California, 70" x 74". Becky's choice of soft colors demonstrates that simple blocks also work well in pastels. As Becky sewed, she saved the leftovers from folded corners. Instead of making a separate "leftovers" project, she sewed these triangles into rows at the top and bottom of her quilt, turning an otherwise square quilt into a rectangular one. Machine quilted by the author.

Materials: 42"-wide fabric

Yardage	Fabric
2½ yds.	Fabric A for blocks and border
3 yds.	Fabric B for blocks and border
1 yd.	Fabric C for blocks
¾ yd.	for binding
4½ yds.	for backing

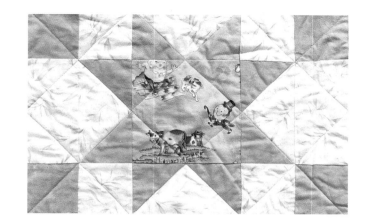

Cutting Chart

FABRIC	STRIP WIDTH	NO. OF STRIPS	CROSSCUT INTO	NO. NEEDED		
				Fair and Square	Stars	Total
Blocks						
A	3½"	14	3½" x 3½"	96	52	148
B	3½"	17	3½" x 6½"	48	52	100
B	3½"	5	3½" x 3½"	48	0	48
C	6½"	5	6½" x 6½"	12	13	25
Borders						
A	3½"	9				
B	2½"	6				
Binding	2¼"	9				

Quilt Assembly

1. Make 13 Fair and Square blocks (page 19).

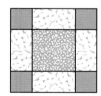

2. Make 12 Sawtooth Star blocks (page 26), but press as shown, so the seams will run in opposite directions when the blocks are sewn together. Reserve the leftovers from the folded corners for the two pieced borders.

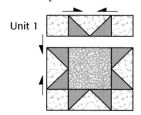

3. Using the illustrations as guides, sew the blocks into 3 rows that start and end with Fair and Square blocks, and 2 rows that start and end with Sawtooth Star blocks. Press the seams in each row toward the Fair and Square blocks.

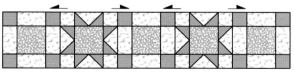

Make 3 rows.

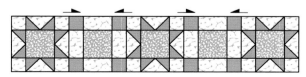

Make 2 rows.

4. Referring to the setting instructions in "Next to Each Other," sew the rows together. Press the seams toward the bottom of the quilt.

5. Referring to the instructions in "Borders" on page 44, sew the 2½" fabric B border strips together end to end, measure the quilt top, and then cut strips to fit the top and bottom edges. Sew one border strip to the top of the quilt and another to the bottom. Press the seams toward the borders.

6. Sew the leftover triangles into squares. Trim each triangle square to 2½" x 2½". Sew these triangle squares into 2 rows of 30 squares each. Then sew one of the rows to the top of the quilt and the other row to the bottom, easing if necessary. Press the seams away from the triangle-square rows.

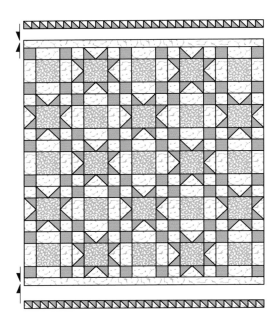

7. Cut fabric B borders for the sides of the quilt, and sew them to the quilt top. Press the seams toward the borders.

8. Sew the fabric A borders to the quilt top, attaching the top and bottom borders first and then the sides, following the procedure used in step 5.

Piecing the Backing

Cut 2 lengths of fabric, each 74" long. Remove the selvages and stitch the fabric together along the 74"-long edges. Press the seams open.

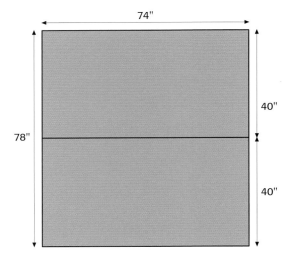

Finishing

Refer to "Finishing Your Quilt" on page 72 for quilting and binding instructions.

Blue Sampler

Setting: Sashings without Cornerstones (pages 39–41)
Size: 46½" x 62"

Blue Sampler made by Ashley Carmichael, age 12, 1998, Fort Leavenworth, Kansas, 46½" x 62".
Ashley created this sampler in weekly sewing sessions. She worked with the author during the early development stages of this book. Ashley is currently living with her family in Egypt. Machine quilted by Ashley.

Materials: 42"-wide fabric

For some of the blocks in this quilt, the Block Workshop instructions call for four fabrics. If you'd like to reproduce the look of the sample quilt, limit yourself to three fabrics.

Yardage	Fabric
¾ yd.	Fabric A (dark blue) for blocks
1½ yds.	Fabric B (pale blue) for blocks
1 yd.	Fabric C (medium blue) for blocks
1¾ yds.	Fabric D for sashing, borders, and blocks
½ yd.	for binding
3 yds.	for backing

Cutting Chart

FABRIC	STRIP WIDTH	NO. OF STRIPS
Sashings and Borders		
D	3½"	13
Binding		
	2¼"	6

NOTE: Cutting instructions for each block can be found in "The Block Workshop" (page 18). See step 1 below for individual block page references. The Railroad Crossing block pattern in this quilt is slightly different from the pattern in "The Block Workshop."

Quilt Assembly

1. Make 1 each of the following blocks:
   Monkey Wrench (page 20)
   Butterfly (page 21)
   House (page 23)
   Indian Hatchet (page 25)
   Sawtooth Star (page 26)
   Basket (page 27)
   King David's Crown (page 27)
   Friendship Star (page 31)
   Pinwheel (page 32)
   Flower (page 32)
   Railroad Crossing (page 36)
   Sailboat (page 38)

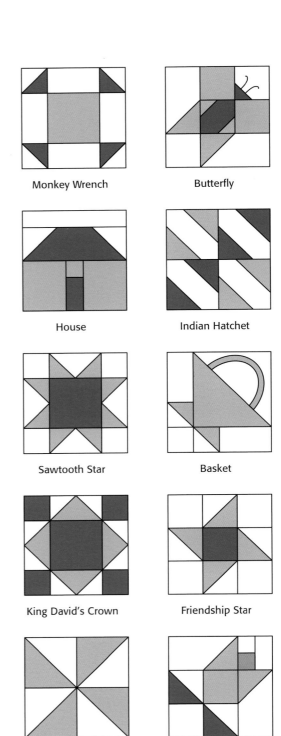

Monkey Wrench

Butterfly

House

Indian Hatchet

Sawtooth Star

Basket

King David's Crown

Friendship Star

Pinwheel

Flower

Railroad Crossing

Sailboat

2. Crosscut 3 of the strips that you cut for sashings and borders to make 8 sashings, each 3½" x 12½".

3. Using the instructions provided in "Sashings without Cornerstones," sew the blocks into 4 rows of 3 blocks each, with vertical sashing strips between the blocks. Press the seams toward the sashing strips.

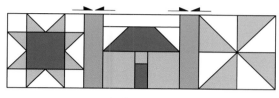

Make 4 rows.

4. Referring to "Sashings without Cornerstones" again, sew the horizontal sashing strips to each row, omitting the bottom row; then sew the rows together. Press the seams toward the sashing strips.

5. To complete the quilt top, follow the instructions provided in "Borders" on page 44.

Piecing the Backing

Measure the width of the quilt across its center and add 4". Cut 2 pieces of backing fabric, each to this length. Sew the pieces together along their long edges and press the seam open. Measure the length of the quilt and add 4". Trim the backing to the length you just calculated.

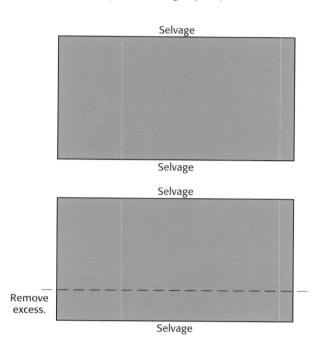

Finishing

Refer to "Finishing Your Quilt" on page 72 for quilting and binding instructions.

Butterflies II

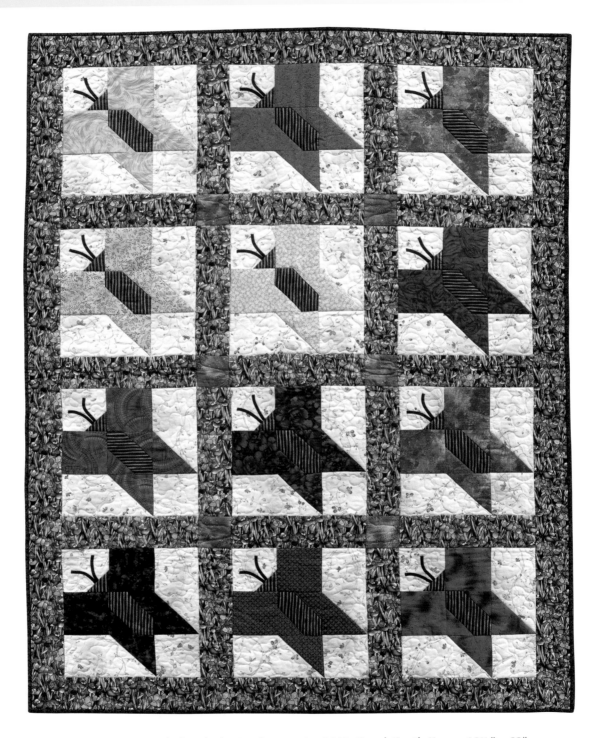

Butterflies II made by Nicole Gonder, age 13, 2000, Seoul, South Korea, 46½" x 62".
Nicole loves bright, clear fabrics. She wanted her butterflies to seem as if they were flying among the flowers.
Machine quilted by Nicole and the author. From the collection of the author.

Materials: 42"-wide fabric

Yardage	Fabric
¼ yd. each (or 5" x 25" scrap) of 12 prints	Fabric A for blocks
1¼ yds.	Fabric B for blocks
½ yd.	Fabric C for blocks
5" x 23" scrap	for cornerstones
1½ yds.	for sashings and borders
½ yd.	for binding
3¼ yds.	for backing

Cutting Chart

FABRIC	STRIP WIDTH	NO. OF STRIPS	CROSSCUT INTO	NO. NEEDED
A (each butterfly)	4½"	1	4½" x 4½"	4
			Then cut 3" x 3"	2
B	4½"	8	4½" x 8½"	24
			4½" x 4½"	12
C	4½"	2	4½" x 4½"	12
	2½"	1	2½" x 2½"	12
Cornerstones	3½"	1	3½" x 3½"	6
Sashings and Borders	3½"	9	3½" x 12½"	17
Binding	2¼"	6		

Quilt Assembly

1. Make 12 Butterfly blocks (page 21).

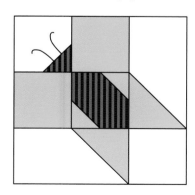

2. Using the instructions provided in "Sashings with Cornerstones," sew the blocks and vertical sashing strips into 4 horizontal rows of 3 blocks each. Press the seams toward the sashing strips.

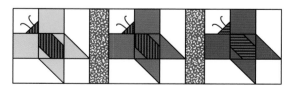

Make 4 rows.

3. Again referring to "Sashings with Cornerstones," add the horizontal sashing-with-cornerstone strips to 3 of the rows. Then sew the rows together.

4. To complete the quilt top, follow the instructions provided in "Borders" on page 44.

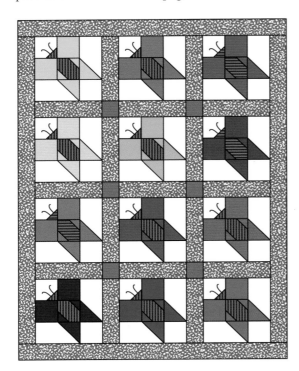

Piecing the Backing

Measure the width of the quilt across its center and add 4". Cut 2 pieces of backing fabric, each to this length. Sew the pieces together along their long edges and press the seam open. Measure the length of the quilt and add 4". Trim the backing to the length you just calculated.

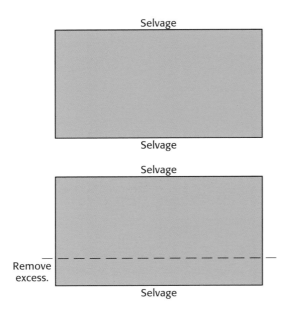

Finishing

Refer to "Finishing Your Quilt" on page 72 for quilting and binding instructions.

SUBSTITUTING BLOCKS

If you're not in the mood for butterflies, just substitute a different block! Patrick Rielly, age 11, used the Leaf block (page 34) to make this autumn-themed quilt. Each time Patrick and the author met to work on this project, which Patrick calls *Fall Leaves*, they debated which new leaf was their favorite. Patrick's mother, Anne Rielly, did the quilting.

Cousins by the Row

Cousins by the Row made by cousins, Anna Martin, age 7; Becky Martin, age 12; Sarah Eikmeier, age 10; David Martin, age 11; and Eric Eikmeier; age 12, 1998, 62½" x 72".
Each cousin sewed a row of this quilt during a summer visit to the family farm. The quilt was later set together by Sarah Eikmeier and machine quilted by the author. The cousins include the author's children and the children of three of the author's brothers. From the collection of the author.

Materials: 42"-wide fabric

Yardage	Fabric
5 different scraps totaling 1¼ yds.	Fabric A for blocks
2½ yds.	Fabric B for blocks
5 different scraps totaling ½ yd.	Fabric C for blocks
⅛ yd.	Fabric D for blocks
5 different scraps totaling ½ yd.	for sashings
½ yd.	for borders
½ yd.	for binding
4 yds.	for backing

Cutting Chart

FABRIC	STRIP WIDTH	NO. OF STRIPS	CROSSCUT INTO	NO. NEEDED
Butterflies				
A	4½"	1	4½" x 4½"	4 from each fabric
A			3½" x 3½"	2 from each fabric
B	4½"	4	4½" x 4½"	10
B			4½" x 8½"	10
C	4½"	1	4½" x 4½"	5 total
Friendship Stars				
A (5 different)	4⅞"	1	4⅞" x 4⅞"	2 from each fabric
B	4⅞"	2	4⅞" x 4⅞"	10
B	4½"	3	4½" x 4½"	20
C	4½"	1	4½" x 4½"	5 total
Baskets				
A	8⅞"		8⅞" x 8⅞"	1 from each fabric
(See instructions for cutting handle on page 28.)				
A	3⅞"		3⅞" x 3⅞"	1 from each fabric
B	3½"	3	3½" x 3½"	5
B			3½" x 6½"	10
B	3⅞"	1	3⅞" x 3⅞"	5
B	8⅞"	1	8⅞" x 8⅞"	3
Pinwheels				
A			6⅞" x 6⅞"	10 (2 for each block)
B			6⅞" x 6⅞"	10 (2 for each block)

FABRIC	STRIP WIDTH	NO. OF STRIPS	CROSSCUT INTO	NO. NEEDED
Flowers				
A	4½"	2	4½" x 4½"	15 total
B	4⅞"	1	4⅞" x 4⅞"	5
B	4½"	3	4½" x 2½"	5
B			4½" x 4½"	5
B			4½" x 8½"	10
B	2½"	1	2½" x 2½"	5
C	4⅞"	1	4⅞" x 4⅞"	5
D	2½"	1	2½" x 2½"	5
Sashing	2½"	1½ from each fabric		
Borders	2½"	6		
Binding	2¼"	6		

Quilt Assembly

1. Make 5 each of the following blocks: Butterfly (page 21), Basket (page 27), Friendship Star (page 31), Pinwheel (page 32), and Flower (page 32).

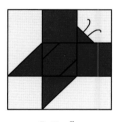
Butterfly

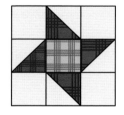
Friendship Star

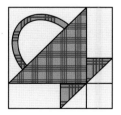
Basket

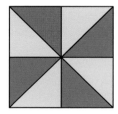
Pinwheel

Flower

2. Sew each set of 5 blocks to form a horizontal row. Press the seams to either side.

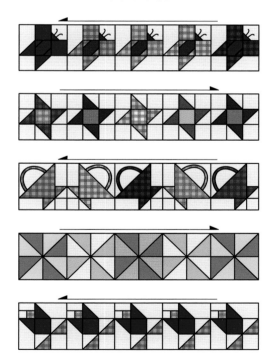

3. Using the instructions provided in "Row by Row," add the horizontal sashing strips to the rows, omitting the bottom row.

4. To complete the quilt top, follow the instructions provided in "Borders" on page 44.

Piecing the Backing

Measure the width of the quilt across its center and add 4". Cut 2 pieces of backing fabric, each to this length. Sew the pieces together along their long edges and press the seam open. Measure the length of the quilt and add 4". Trim the backing to the length you just calculated.

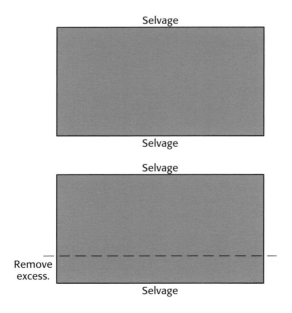

Selvage

Selvage

Selvage

Remove excess.

Selvage

Finishing

Refer to "Finishing Your Quilt" on page 72 for quilting and binding instructions.

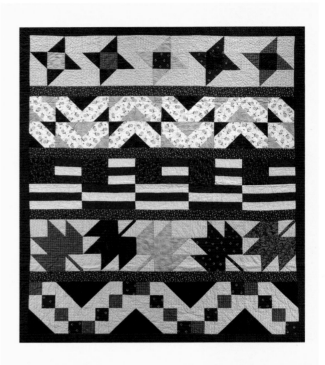

MIXING AND MATCHING BLOCKS

You can make a lot of different row-by-row quilts by mixing and matching blocks. Ten-year-old Kate Mock made this fun project, which she calls *Follow the Yellow Brick Road,* by combining Friendship Star, Indian Hatchet, Flag, Leaf, and Railroad Crossing blocks. An independent quilt-maker, Kate barely had the binding sewn on before she was planning her next project. *Follow the Yellow Brick Road* was machine quilted by Kate's mother, Tracy Mock.

Irish Chain

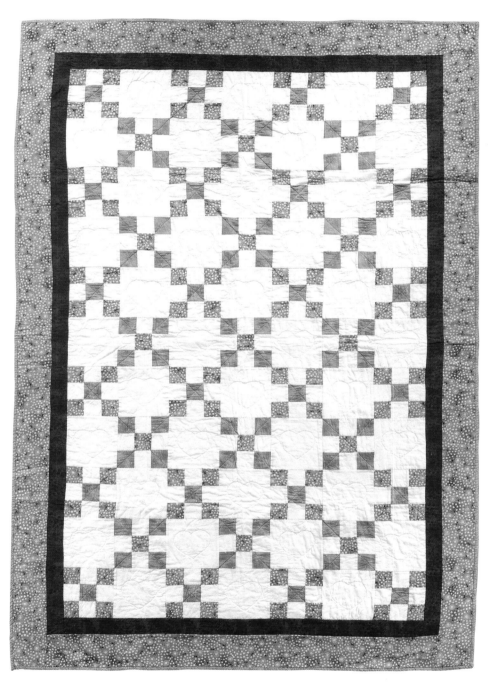

Irish Chain made by Rachel Capra, age 14, 2000, Seoul, South Korea, 52½" x 76".
Rachel saw a Single Irish Chain quilt that inspired her color placement in this very traditional
design. Portions of blocks are added along the bottom and one side to balance the design.
Instead of making individual blocks, Rachel constructed the quilt in rows, thereby speeding
up the quilt's assembly. Hand and machine quilted by Rachel.

Materials: 42"-wide fabric

Yardage	Fabric
¾ yd.	Fabric A for blocks
2 yds.	Fabric B for blocks
¾ yd.	Fabric C for blocks
½ yd.	for border 1
1 yd.	for border 2
½ yd.	for binding
3½ yds.	for backing

Cutting Chart

FABRIC	STRIP WIDTH	NO. OF STRIPS	CROSSCUT INTO	NO. NEEDED
A	2½"	10	2½" x 2½"	156
B	2½"	9	2½" x 2½"	132
B	6½"	7	6½" x 6½"	38
C	2½"	9	2½" x 2½"	129
Border 1	2½"	6		
Border 2	4"	8		
Binding	2¼"	8		

Quilt Assembly

NOTE: The color placement in this quilt differs from the placement described in "The Block Workshop" instructions. Also, instead of sewing this quilt together in 12" blocks, you'll sew portions of blocks into horizontal, 6"-wide rows, and then sew the rows together. Note also that the overall quilt design includes additional squares along one vertical edge and along the bottom. Double Nine Patch blocks are asymmetrical; without the added squares, the quilt would look unbalanced.

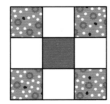

Nine-patch unit from
Double Nine Patch

1. Make 24 nine-patch units (Unit 1, page 18) with the 2½" squares of fabrics A, B, and C. Refer to the illustrations for correct color placement.

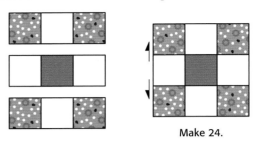

Make 24.

2. Make 15 more nine-patch units with the 2½" squares of fabrics A, B, and C, referring to the illustrations for color placement. Note that the placement of the A and C squares is opposite to that in the nine-patch units you made in step 1.

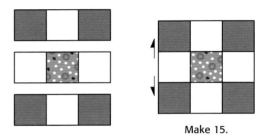

Make 15.

3. Using the illustrations as placement guides, sew the units you made in steps 1 and 2 into rows, alternating them with the 6½" squares of fabric B. Press the seams toward the 6½" squares.

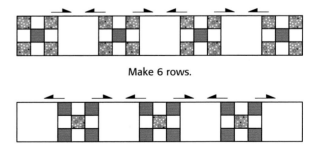

Make 6 rows.

Make 5 rows.

4. Sew the rows together, referring to the photograph on page 59 for placement. Press the seams toward the bottom of the quilt.

5. To complete the quilt top, follow the instructions provided in "Borders" on page 44.

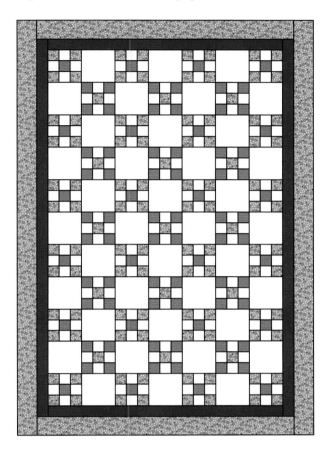

Piecing the Backing

Measure the width of the quilt across its center and add 4". Cut 2 pieces of backing fabric, each to this length. Sew the pieces together along their long edges and press the seam open. Measure the length of the quilt and add 4". Trim the backing to the length you just calculated.

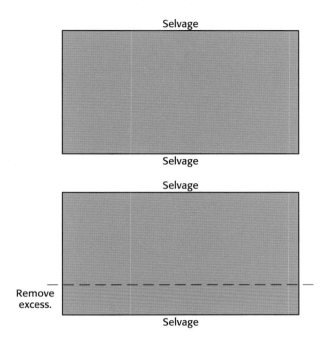

Finishing

Refer to "Finishing Your Quilt" on page 72 for quilting and binding instructions.

Patch Quilt

SETTING: SASHINGS WITH CORNERSTONES (PAGES 41–42)
SIZE: 46½" x 62"

Patch Quilt made by Sarah Eikmeier, age 11, 2000, Seoul, South Korea, 46½" x 62".
Sarah, like many children, has collected souvenir patches from places she's visited and events she's attended. To provide settings for her collection of patches, she chose blocks with large center squares. By changing the color placement or corners, Sarah created four different blocks from two patterns. (Many traditional blocks are based on slight variations of other blocks—variations that give them totally different looks.) Machine quilted by the author.

NOTE: Sarah chose blocks that had large center squares to which she could attach her patches. You can use this same concept to feature special fabrics instead.

Materials: 42"-wide fabric

Yardage	Fabric
⅔ yd.	Fabric A for blocks and cornerstones
1¼ yds.	Fabric B for blocks
1 yd.	Fabric C for blocks
1½ yds.	for sashing and borders
½ yd.	for binding
3 yds.	for backing

Cutting Chart

FABRIC	STRIP WIDTH	NO. OF STRIPS	CROSSCUT INTO	NO. NEEDED
A	6½"	2	6½" x 6½"	12
B	3⅞"	1	3⅞" x 3⅞"	6
B	3½"	6	3½" x 6½"	36
B	3½"	3	3½" x 3½"	24
C	3⅞"	1	3⅞" x 3⅞"	6
C	3½"	6	3½" x 3½"	58
C	3½"	2	3½" x 6½"	12
Sashings	12½"	1	12½" x 3½"	11
Sashings	3½"	2	3½" x 12½"	6
Borders	3½"	6		
Cornerstones	3½"	1	3½" x 3½"	8

Quilt Assembly

1. Make 3 Sawtooth Star blocks (page 26).

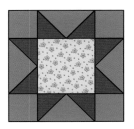

2. Make 3 King David's Crown blocks (page 27) by changing the color placement in the Sawtooth Stars.

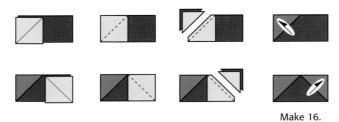

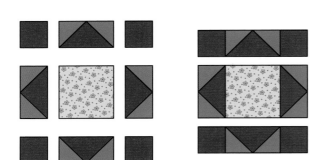

Make 16.

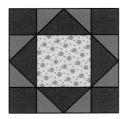

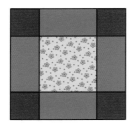

3. Make 3 Fair and Square blocks (page 19).

4. Referring to the illustrations below, make 3 Monkey Wrench blocks (page 20) by replacing the corners of the Fair and Square blocks with three-step triangle squares (page 13). Use the 3⅞" squares of fabrics A and B for the three-step triangle squares.

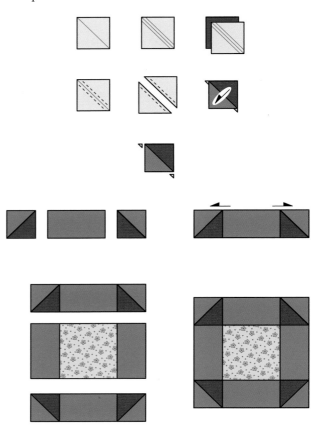

5. Sew a souvenir patch to the center of each block.
6. Using the instructions provided in "Sashings with Cornerstones" and the illustration provided here, assemble and sew the blocks, sashing strips, and cornerstones.

7. To complete the quilt top, follow the instructions provided in "Borders" on page 44.

Piecing the Backing

Measure the width of the quilt across its center and add 4". Cut 2 pieces of backing fabric, each to this length. Sew the pieces together along their long edges and press the seam open. Measure the length of the quilt and add 4". Trim the backing to the length you just calculated.

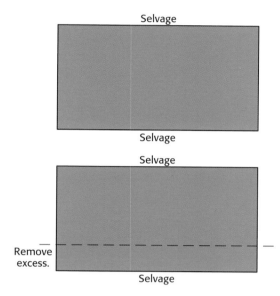

Finishing

Refer to "Finishing Your Quilt" on page 72 for quilting and binding instructions.

Leftovers by Sarah Eikmeier, age 11, 2000, Seoul, South Korea.

Ranger's Cabin

Ranger's Cabin made by Eric Eikmeier, age 12, 1999, Fort Leavenworth, Kansas, 52" x 73".
Eric made his quilt after a family camping trip to Yellowstone National Park. The striped batik fabric
reminded him of the trees that remained in the park after a major forest fire. One of the rangers told
Eric that he'd spent twenty-five summers living in the park and giving trail talks to visitors. Eric was
impressed enough to give the ranger his own cabin in this quilt. Machine quilted by the author.

Materials: 42"-wide fabric

Yardage	Fabric
1 ¼ yds.	Fabric A for blocks
2 ¼ yds.	Fabric B for blocks
⅓ yd.	Fabric C for blocks
1 ½ yds.	for sashings and borders
½ yd.	for binding
3 ½ yds.	for backing

Cutting Chart

FABRIC	STRIP WIDTH	NO. OF STRIPS	CROSSCUT INTO	NO. NEEDED
A	4½"	7	4½" x 12½"	19
A	4⅞"	3	4⅞" x 4⅞"	19
B	4⅞"	3	4⅞" x 4⅞"	19
B	4½"	13	4½" x 4½"	40
B			4½" x 5½"	38
B			4½" x 2½"	38
C	4½"	2	2½" x 4½"	19
House			5½" x 6½"	2
			2½" x 2½"	1
Door			2½" x 4½"	1
Roof			4½" x 12½"	1
Grass			2½" x 12½"	1
Sashing and Borders	3½"	11		
Binding	2¼"	7		

Quilt Assembly

1. Make 19 Pine Tree blocks (page 35), but be sure to press the seams as shown.

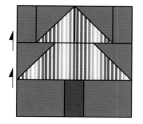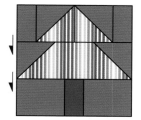

Press 9 blocks.   Press 10 blocks.

2. Make 1 House block (page 23).

3. Using the instructions provided in "Row by Row," sew the blocks together to make 5 rows of 4 blocks each. As you do this, arrange the Pine Tree blocks in each row so that the direction in which their seams are pressed alternates. And be sure to place the House block in the correct position!

4. Again referring to the instructions in "Row by Row," sew horizontal sashing strips to every row except the one at the bottom, and then sew the rows together. Press the seams toward the sashing strips.

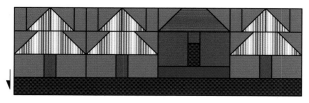

Make 1 row.

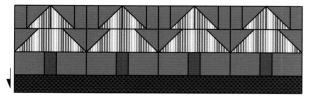

Make 4 rows.

5. To complete the quilt top, follow the instructions provided in "Borders" on page 44.

Piecing the Backing

Measure the width of the quilt across its center and add 4". Cut 2 pieces of backing fabric, each to this length. Sew the pieces together along their long edges and press the seam open. Measure the length of the quilt and add 4". Trim the backing to the length you just calculated.

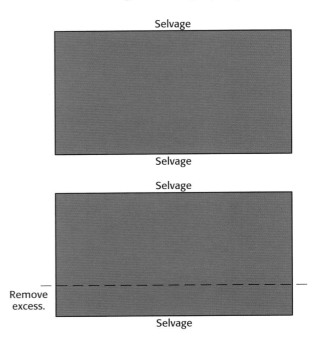

Finishing

Refer to "Finishing Your Quilt" on page 72 for quilting and binding instructions.

Sarah's Sampler

SETTING: SASHINGS WITHOUT CORNERSTONES
(PAGES 39–41)
SIZE: 42" X 56"

Sarah's Sampler made by Sarah Bryant, age 8, 2000, Seoul, South Korea, 42" x 56". Sarah chose a limited palette of fabrics and six of her favorite blocks for this quilt. She then reversed the color placement for a second set of blocks to complete a twelve-block sampler. Sarah's quilt is hand pieced and hand quilted; she completed much of the work independently.

Materials: 42"-wide fabric

For some of the blocks in this quilt, the Block Workshop instructions call for four fabrics. If you'd like to reproduce the look of the sample quilt, limit yourself to three fabrics.

Yardage	Fabric
¾ yd.	Fabric A for blocks
1½ yds.	Fabric B for blocks
¾ yd.	Fabric C for blocks
1½ yds.	for sashings and borders
½ yd.	for binding
3½ yds.	for backing

NOTE: Cutting instructions for each block can be found in "The Block Workshop" (page 18). See step 1 in "Quilt Assembly" at right for specific page references.

Quilt Assembly

1. Make 2 each of the following blocks, adding variety by reversing the color placement for one of each type: Flag (page 20), Butterfly (page 21), House (page 23), Pinwheel (page 32), Flower (page 32), and Sailboat (page 38). See below.
2. Using the instructions provided in "Sashings without Cornerstones," sew the blocks into 4 rows of 3 blocks each, with vertical sashing strips sewn between the blocks. Press the seams toward the sashing strips. Then sew the horizontal sashing strips to each row.

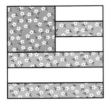 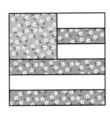

Flag

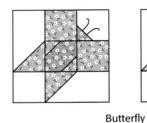

Butterfly

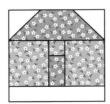 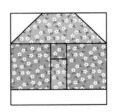

House

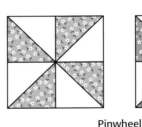

Pinwheel

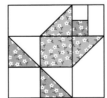 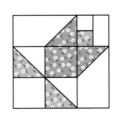

Flower

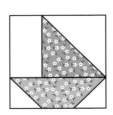 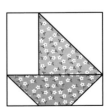

Sailboat

3. Using the illustration of the quilt, sew the rows together. Press the seams toward the sashing strips.

4. To complete the quilt top, follow the instructions provided in "Borders" on page 44.

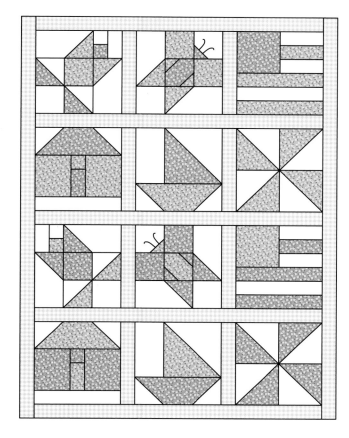

Piecing the Backing

Measure the width of the quilt across its center and add 4". Cut 2 pieces of backing fabric, each to this length. Sew the pieces together along their long edges and press the seam open. Measure the length of the quilt and add 4". Trim the backing to the length you just calculated.

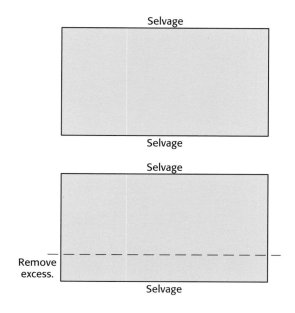

Finishing

Refer to "Finishing Your Quilt" on page 72 for quilting and binding instructions.

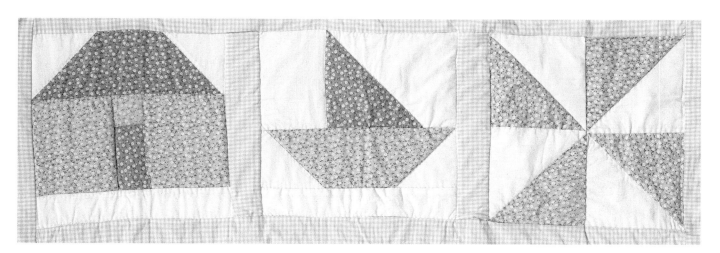

Finishing Your Quilt

 Before layering and basting your quilt, you must decide how you want to finish its edges, so read "Finishing the Edges" (page 74) before you continue. If you choose to add an applied binding (page 76), you'll start by using the step-by-step instructions in this section to baste the three layers together. Then you'll complete the quilting, and finally, you'll attach the binding. For right-sides-together finishing (page 74), you'll sew together the outer edges of the quilt and the backing, right sides together. Next, you'll turn the quilt right side out. Then you'll baste it and quilt it. If you'll be sending your quilt out for edge-to-edge machine quilting, basting may not be required. Check with your quilter to be sure.

Basting

Basting holds the three layers—quilt top, batting, and backing—together temporarily until you complete the quilting. Generally, when my students machine quilt, they pin-baste with 1" safety pins; when they hand quilt, they baste with thread.

To baste a quilt that will have an applied binding:
1. Lay the backing, on the floor or on another large surface, wrong side up.
2. With packing tape, securely tape the backing fabric to the surface, stretching the fabric taut as you do.
3. Smooth the batting over the backing fabric.
4. Smooth the quilt top, right side up, over the batting.

5. Baste the layers together. If you're using safety pins, place them at 5" intervals across the quilt top's entire surface. (Use plenty of pins!) If you're basting with thread, baste a grid of 5" to 6" squares, as shown in the illustration.

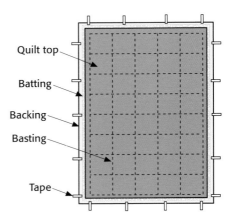

Quilting

Quilting may be performed by hand or machine. If your students don't have access to machines, you'll need to teach them hand quilting. If they do have machines and if they show an aptitude for machine stitching, you may want to instruct them in the basics of machine quilting, too.

Hand Quilting

This book doesn't include instructions for hand quilting, but the following tips may be helpful to you if you want to teach your students the hand-quilting process.

When I started teaching hand quilting to children, I taught them to work with one hand on top and one underneath—the method that most adult quiltmakers use. I quickly realized that this method wouldn't work with children, however, because they didn't want to prick their fingers as they stitched! They couldn't master small stitches, and I was frustrated because I didn't know how to teach them. The answer to this problem came to me while I was at the Museum of the American Quilter in Paducah, Kentucky. There I viewed a quilt made with tiny, perfect stitches by Janice Streeter. In her artist's statement, she said that she quilted with both hands on top. Although I still don't know exactly how Janice does this, her statement was the inspiration that I needed. I went home and figured out a way for the kids to quilt with both hands on top.

My solution requires having my students stitch their quilts while the quilts rest flat on a table, without hoops. We use size 7 embroidery needles, colorful quilting thread, and spoons—in much the same way some quiltmakers used spoons to baste their quilts. Although quilting this way is slow work (you can only take one stitch at a time), my students can often achieve small, even stitches. When working with beginners, I let them take stitches that come to them naturally; sometimes these stitches are huge! After the students have practiced using spoons, I encourage them to take smaller stitches.

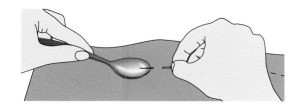

Some students don't like using a spoon, so I let them try quilting without them, even though their stitches won't be as small. As their sewing skills develop and as smaller stitches become more important to them, I encourage them to try a spoon again.

When your students hand quilt with spoons, have them spread out their basted quilts on flat, scratch-resistant surfaces such as Formica tabletops or old rotary-cutting mats; sharp needles will mar other surfaces. Sheets of poster board also work well. Among the materials that I know *won't* work are flannel-backed tablecloths (we sewed a quilt to one!), magazines (they slide around too easily), and newspapers (they're too easy to sew into, and they leave ink on your hands and the quilt).

Machine Quilting

If students are at all interested in sewing machines, chances are they'll want to try machine quilting. I cover a few basics here, but several good publications are available that provide in-depth studies of machine quilting. Use a walking foot attachment for machine-guided quilt-ing, and a darning foot—with the feed dogs lowered—for free-motion quilting.

I was first surprised by how well a student could machine quilt while I was at Fort Campbell, Kentucky. I was scheduled to share the quilting process with a high school sewing class there. On the day of my visit, the teacher was ill, so I couldn't divide the class into two groups as I'd planned. The teacher wanted me to demonstrate machine quilting, but neither of us thought the students could machine quilt successfully on their own.

After my demonstration, in an attempt to get out of work while her teacher was absent, one student decided she'd try machine quilting. I knew that she was "testing" me; I encouraged her to sit down and give the machine a try, but I didn't expect her to succeed. On her first attempt, however, she quilted her name beautifully! After that, I started to encourage my students to try machine quilting. While free-motion machine quilting isn't for everyone, you shouldn't assume that just because some adults find it difficult that children will, too.

1. Place the basted quilt under the needle where you wish to begin quilting. While holding the top thread, lower the needle with the handwheel and take 1 stitch.
2. Pull the bobbin thread to the top by giving the top thread a quick tug.
3. Pull both threads between the toes of the presser foot, so they extend straight out behind the needle.

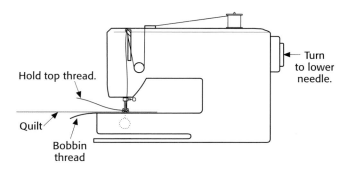

Hold top thread.

Turn to lower needle.

Quilt

Bobbin thread

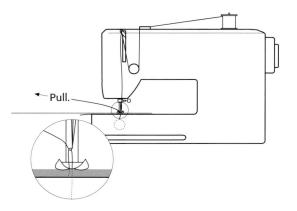

Pull.

4. Lower the presser foot and set the stitch length to "0" so the quilt won't move under the needle. Then lock the thread by stitching in place for a few stitches.

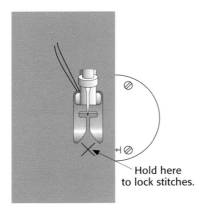

Hold here to lock stitches.

5. If you're stitching with a walking foot, reset the stitch length to about ten stitches per inch and begin stitching the quilting line. If you're free-motion quilting, leave the stitch length set at "0" and quilt by using your hands to move the quilt under the needle.

6. To end the stitching, again hold the quilt firmly to lock the stitches in place. Lift the presser foot, withdraw the quilt, and clip the threads close to its front and back. Clip the tail threads left at the beginning of the quilting.

Quilting with Help

Some students just don't like to quilt. There's nothing wrong with helping them! They won't take any less pride in their projects; they'll be delighted to have their quilts finished. Mothers, aunts, or even professional machine-quilting services can be called upon to finish a quilt. If the quilt is being made for a judged or graded project, however, be sure that all requirements are met. The quilt may automatically fall into a different category if someone other than the maker did the quilting.

Finishing the Edges

There are two ways you can finish the edges on your quilt; both are described in this section. The traditional method is to apply binding to the edges after the quilting process. Some kids find this a bit tedious. An easier method is "right-sides-together finishing." (See the next section.) Keep in mind that when you add a binding, you baste and quilt your layers first. With the right-sides-together finishing method, you sew the layers together around the perimeter before you baste and quilt.

Right-Sides-Together Finishing

With this method, you sew the quilt top and backing, right sides together, around their outer edges, leaving an opening through which the quilt and backing can be turned right side out. You may sew the batting in at the same time, or add it before turning the quilt right side out. You'll do the quilting after the quilt is turned.

For children who want to finish their quilts entirely on their own, using this method eliminates the need to hand stitch an applied binding. Once the quilt is turned, it looks tidy and the batting is contained inside.

To keep the batting (especially a polyester batting) from shifting, after you've turned the quilt, baste it with safety pins or large basting stitches.

1. Cut and piece the backing, making it a little larger than the quilt top. Cut the batting to the same size as the quilt backing.

2. On a large, flat surface, place the quilt top on top of the backing, with their right sides together. Carefully pin all the way around the edges, keeping the 2 layers smooth. (If you'd like to stitch the batting to the top, rather than add it after the quilt has been stitched, spread the batting on the flat surface; place the backing on top of it, right side up; and place the quilt on the backing, right side down. Whenever I sew the batting in this manner, I use a walking foot attachment on my machine.)

3. Leaving a ¼" seam allowance, stitch around all 4 sides, pivoting at the corners and leaving a 12" to 15" opening on one end for turning. Backstitch at the beginning and end of the stitching.

4. Trim each corner at an angle to reduce the bulk, but be careful not to trim too close to the stitching. Trim the backing even with the quilt top.

5. On a flat surface, spread out the stitched quilt top and backing, as shown in the illustration, with the quilt top face up and the backing face down. Unless you've already stitched the batting to the quilt top, arrange it neatly on the quilt top now.

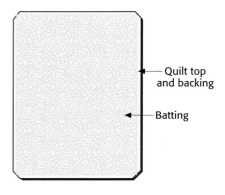

Quilt top and backing

Batting

6. Beginning with the end that is opposite the opening, fold down the 2 corners as shown in the illustration; then roll the quilt up toward the opening. (When turning a large quilt this way, it's easiest to have 1 person at each of the 4 corners.)

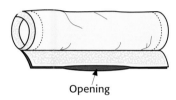

Roll corners first.

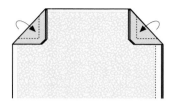

Opening

7. Turn the opening over the rolled-up quilt and push the quilt through the opening. Then unroll the quilt; it will now be right side out, with the batting inside. (If you'd like to practice rolling and turning the quilt, just use a pillowcase and a scrap of batting.)

Push the roll through opening.

8. Using a chopstick or the eraser end of a pencil, reach through the opening and push out the 4 corners.
9. Pin the opening closed, tucking the seam allowances neatly inside. Then blindstitch the opening to close it.
10. Pin or thread-baste to keep the layers from shifting. (See "Basting" on page 72.)
11. Quilt by hand or machine. (See "Quilting" on page 72.)

Blindstitching

Following are instructions for the blind stitch. My students have nicknamed this stitch the "tunnel stitch"; you'll soon see why!

1. Insert the needle so the knot in the thread will be hidden inside the quilt.

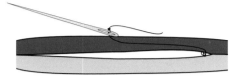

Knot hidden inside

2. Imagine the 2 folded edges at the opening as "tunnels." Place the point of the needle inside either tunnel and scoot it forward about ¼". Then push the point of the needle up through the fabric and out of the tunnel, pulling the thread through.
3. Insert the needle into the tunnel on the other side of the opening, directly across from where it came out on the first side. Scoot the needle through the tunnel to take another stitch.

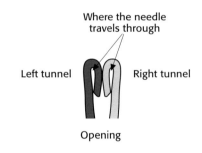

Where the needle travels through

Left tunnel   Right tunnel

Opening

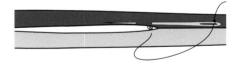

4. Continue stitching, alternating from one tunnel to the other with each stitch, until the opening is completely stitched.

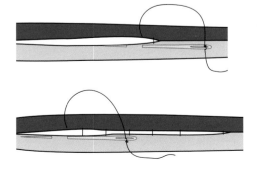

5. At the end of the opening, pull the thread taut so the stitches pull the fabric together and close the opening. Watch as the stitches you've taken disappear. Now you know where the name "blind stitch" came from!

6. Loop the needle around the thread to make a knot. Then pull the needle through, making sure the knot is close to the stitching.

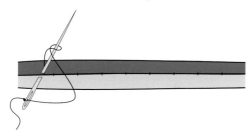

7. Insert the needle near the knot and pull the thread through.

8. Clip the thread close to the fabric.

You can use the same basic blind stitch to sew on an applied binding or to sew the appliquéd handle in the Basket block (page 27). The only difference is that in these two situations, you'll have a tunnel on only one side. The other side will be the flat surface of the back of the quilt or the quilt block. "Tunnel stitch" through the tunnel, cross directly over and take a stitch in the flat side; then cross back to the tunnel for another stitch.

Applied Bindings

An applied binding gives a finished quilt a lovely, polished look; the extra work required is well worth the result. Students who like blindstitching are undaunted by the task of hand sewing all the way around the outside edges of their quilt, but others—including my daughter—can't bear the amount of work required! Children who don't want to complete the hand stitching themselves can get help from an adult.

1. Measure the 4 edges of the quilt and add these measurements together. Add an extra 5". Divide the total by 40 (the width in inches of the fabric from which the binding is cut). Now round up to the nearest whole number. Cut this number of binding strips.

2. Cut the ends of the binding strips at 45° angles, and seam them end to end to make a long strip. Press the seams open.

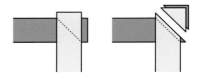

3. Press the binding strip in half along its entire length, with its wrong sides together. Turn under ¼" of one end.

Fold line

4. Complete all quilting by hand or machine.

5. Trim the outer edges of the quilt with a rotary cutter and ruler, leaving the edges straight and even.

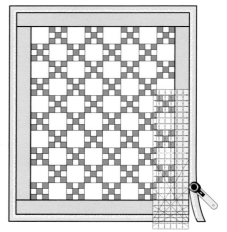

Trim outside edges.

6. Working on the front of the quilt and starting halfway along one edge, pin the binding in place as shown in the illustration. (Start with the binding end that you turned under.) Use a walking foot attachment on your machine and leave a ¼" seam allowance.

7. Begin sewing about 2" in from the end of the binding strip.
8. Sew almost to the corner of the quilt, stopping ¼" from the quilt edge. Backstitch and cut the threads.

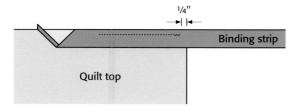

Quilt top

Binding strip

¼"

9. Rotate the quilt, so the edge you just stitched is now at the top and the edge you'll sew next is at the right. The binding is still attached—don't cut it!
10. Fold the binding up as shown in the illustration, keeping it aligned with the edge that you'll sew next.

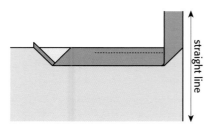

straight line

11. Fold the binding down so that the fold is even with the top edge. Pin the binding in place along the right-hand edge of the quilt.

Fold even with top edge.

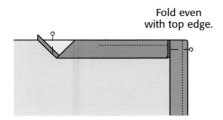

12. Begin stitching at the corner of the quilt and continue until you're ¼" from the next corner. Backstitch, cut the threads, and rotate the quilt again.
13. Continue until you've stitched the binding around all 4 edges and have almost reached the binding's "beginning tail." Trim the ending tail so that it's long enough to overlap the beginning tail but not so long that it covers the beginning stitches.

14. Open the folded beginning tail and tuck the ending tail into it. Pin in place, and stitch, backstitching at the end.

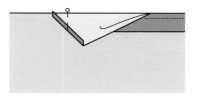

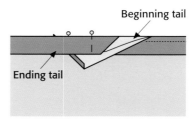

Beginning tail

Ending tail

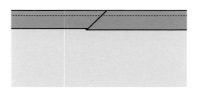

15. Turn the folded edge of the binding to the back of the quilt; as you do this, the corners will automatically miter themselves. Make sure the folded edge just covers the stitching on the back. Don't bring it too far to the back, but don't leave the stitching exposed either. Blindstitch the binding to the back of the quilt.

Quilt back

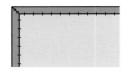

Making a Hanging Sleeve

The preferred method for hanging quilts is with hanging sleeves. In fact, many quilt exhibits require them. When I make one of these sleeves, I use the same fabric that I used for the backing because doing so makes the sleeve less obvious.

1. Cut the sleeve fabric at least 6" wide. Piece strips together, if necessary, to make the strip as long as the width of the quilt.

NOTE: A 6-inch starting strip yields a sleeve that is about 2¾" wide. Some quilt exhibitions request a 4" wide sleeve, which means you'd need to start with an 8½"-wide fabric strip. If you plan to show a quilt in an exhibition, double-check their requirements before adding a sleeve.

2. Turn under a ¼" hem on each short end and press. Turn under again to enclose the raw edges, and press again. Sew each hem with thread that matches the fabric.

3. Fold the strip in half along its length, with the wrong sides together and the raw edges aligned. Stitch the raw edges together, leaving a ¼" seam allowance.

4. Rotate the tube so its seam is at the back. Mark the tube's center and match it to the center of the quilt, along the upper edge of the quilt back. The sleeve will be slightly shorter than your quilt is wide. Pin the tube in place, just below the binding. Then blindstitch both long edges to the backing.

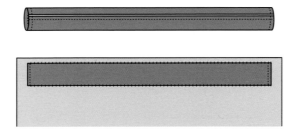

5. Insert a dowel or rod into the hanging sleeve. Suspend the dowel on wall brackets or rest it on 2 nails in the wall.

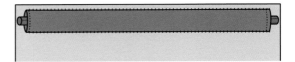

Signing Your Quilt

A quilt isn't finished until it's been signed. If your quilt backing is light in color, you may want to sign directly on its surface. If the backing fabric is a busy print or dark in color, attach a label to a lower back corner of the quilt. Include the maker's name and age, the city and state in which the quilt was made, and the date. If the quilting was done by someone other than the maker, add the appropriate information.

Use a permanent pen to write on a pre-printed label; these labels are widely available from fabric manufacturers.

Alternatively, you can make your own label. Use pinking shears to cut out a piece of fabric and stitch it directly to the quilt without further finishing of the edge, or cut out the label shape, turn its raw edges to the back, press them, and then sew the label in place. Use a blind stitch or running stitch that won't go all the way through to the front of the quilt.

Washing Your Quilt

I wash all my quilts when they're finished because I love the way the fabrics and batting nestle together after laundering. The initial washing also removes dirt and quilting markings.

1. Fill the washing machine with warm water. Add a mild soap, such as Orvus Quilt Soap, which is available at local quilt and fabric stores. Agitate the machine to mix the soap and water.
2. Turn the machine off, submerge the quilt, and wash it by hand.
3. Turn the machine on to spin and drain the wash water.
4. Remove the quilt and let the machine fill with rinse water.
5. Submerge the quilt and rinse it by hand. One or more rinses (and spin cycles) may be required to remove all the soap.
6. Place the quilt in the dryer and set the dryer on low. Remove the quilt before it's completely dry and allow it to air dry either on a wash line or by laying it flat.

About the Author

Barbara J. Eikmeier grew up on a dairy farm in Northern California. Like many people in her farm community, she and her eight brothers and sisters participated in 4-H. There she learned to sew, and when she was fourteen, Barbara received her first sewing machine. Although she experimented with quilting as a teenager, she didn't begin quilting in earnest until 1984. Barbara has been teaching quilting to adults and children since 1990.

Frequent military moves with her husband, Dale, have exposed Barbara to a variety of quilting activities. It was a military assignment at the isolated desert army post of Fort Irwin, California, that led her to teach quilting to children. Educated as a nurse, Barbara has made quilting her career, teaching and lecturing wherever the army sends her husband and family.

Barbara belongs to The American Quilt Study Group; The American Quilter's Society; Kaw Valley Quilters Guild, Lawrence, Kansas; and Happy Quilters, Seoul, South Korea. She currently lives in Seoul with her husband; her children, Eric and Sarah; and their usual entourage of pets.

NEW AND BESTSELLING TITLES FROM

America's Best-Loved Craft & Hobby Books™

America's Best-Loved Quilt Books®

QUILTING
From That Patchwork Place, an imprint of Martingale & Company

Appliqué
Artful Appliqué
Colonial Appliqué
Red and Green: An Appliqué Tradition
Rose Sampler Supreme
Your Family Heritage: Projects in
   Appliqué

Baby Quilts
Appliqué for Baby
The Quilted Nursery
Quilts for Baby: Easy as ABC
More Quilts for Baby: Easy as ABC
Even More Quilts for Baby: Easy as ABC

Holiday Quilts
Easy and Fun Christmas Quilts
Favorite Christmas Quilts from That
   Patchwork Place
Paper Piece a Merry Christmas
A Snowman's Family Album Quilt
Welcome to the North Pole

Learning to Quilt
Basic Quiltmaking Techniques for:
   Borders and Bindings
   Curved Piecing
   Divided Circles
   Eight-Pointed Stars
   Hand Appliqué
   Machine Appliqué
   Strip Piecing
The Joy of Quilting
The Quilter's Handbook
Your First Quilt Book (or it should be!)

Paper Piecing
50 Fabulous Paper-Pieced Stars
A Quilter's Ark
Easy Machine Paper Piecing
Needles and Notions
Paper-Pieced Curves
Show Me How to Paper Piece

Rotary Cutting
101 Fabulous Rotary-Cut Quilts
365 Quilt Blocks a Year Perpetual
   Calendar
Fat Quarter Quilts
Lap Quilting Lives!
Quick Watercolor Quilts
Quilts from Aunt Amy
Spectacular Scraps
Time-Crunch Quilts

Small & Miniature Quilts
Bunnies By The Bay Meets Little Quilts
Celebrate! with Little Quilts
Easy Paper-Pieced Miniatures
Little Quilts All Through the House

CRAFTS
From Martingale & Company

300 Papermaking Recipes
The Art of Handmade Paper and
   Collage
The Art of Stenciling
Creepy Crafty Halloween
Gorgeous Paper Gifts
Grow Your Own Paper
Stamp with Style
Wedding Ribbonry

KNITTING
From Martingale & Company

Comforts of Home
Fair Isle Sweaters Simplified
Knit It Your Way
Simply Beautiful Sweaters
Two Sticks and a String
The Ultimate Knitter's Guide
Welcome Home: Kaffe Fassett

COLLECTOR'S COMPASS™
From Martingale & Company

20th Century Glass
'50s Decor
Barbie® Doll
Jewelry

Coming to *Collector's Compass* Spring 2001:

20th Century Dinnerware
American Coins
Movie Star Collectibles
'60s Decor